This book belongs to
Ninja
Nico

Read more in the Ninja Nani series
Ninja Nani and the Bumbling Burglars
Ninja Nani and the Zapped Zombie Kids

Read more for middle grade from Duckbill
Against All Odds by Ramendra Kumar
The Case of the Candy Bandit by Archit Taneja
The Case of the Careless Aliens by Archit Taneja
Oops the Mighty Gurgle by RamG Vallath
The Deadly Royal Recipe by Ranjit Lal
Vanamala and the Cephalopod by Shalini Srinivasan
The White Zone by Carolyn Marsden
Flat-track Bullies by Balaji Venkataramanan
Ravana Refuses to Die by Rustom Dadachanji
Dhanak by Anushka Ravishankar and Nagesh Kukunoor
Simply Nanju by Zainab Sulaiman
Hot Chocolate is Thicker than Blood by Rupa Gulab
The Sherlock Holmes Connection by Martin Widmark, Anushka Ravishankar, Katarina Genar and Bikram Ghosh
Tiger Boy by Mitali Perkins
The Hill School Girls: Alone by A. Coven
The Hill School Girls: Secrets by A. Coven
The Hill School Girls: Strangers by A. Coven
The Hill School Girls: Trouble by A. Coven
Pops! by Balaji Venkataramanan
Neha and the Nose by Ruchika Chanana
Karma Fights a Monster by Evan Purcell
Karma Meets a Zombie by Evan Purcell
The Piano by Nandita Basu

Read more by Lavanya Karthik from Duckbill
Neel on Wheels

NINJA NANI

& THE MAD MUMMY MIX-UP

To our favourite NINJA NICO, the greatest ninja in the Ninja business!

Muah Muah Muah!
Merry Xmas
— Sujay
GOA DEC '23

LAVANYA KARTHIK

duckbill

An imprint of Penguin Random House

DUCKBILL BOOKS
USA | Canada | UK | Ireland | Australia
New Zealand | India | South Africa | China

Duckbill Books is part of the Penguin Random House group of companies
whose addresses can be found at global.penguinrandomhouse.com

Published by Penguin Random House India Pvt. Ltd
4th Floor, Capital Tower 1, MG Road,
Gurugram 122 002, Haryana, India

Penguin
Random House
India

First published by Duckbill Books 2018

This edition published in Duckbill Books by Penguin Random House India 2020

Copyright © Lavanya Karthik 2018

Lavanya Karthik asserts the moral right to be identified
as the author of this work

All right reserved

10 9 8 7 6 5 4 3 2

ISBN 9789383331901

Typeset by PrePSol Enterprises Pvt. Ltd.
Printed at Repro India Limited

This book is sold subject to the condition that it shall not, by way of trade
or otherwise, be lent, resold, hired out, or otherwise circulated without the
publisher's prior consent in any form of binding or cover other than that in
which it is published and without a similar condition including this condition
being imposed on the subsequent purchaser.

www.penguin.co.in

MIX
Paper from
responsible sources
FSC® C047271

You need to read this before
One

You know how Deepu's Nani became Ninja Nani, right? Well, if you need reminding, let Deepu tell you himself ...

This is Deepu. (HI)	This is Nani. (GRRR)	Nani was just like any other granny until one day...
ZZZAP! (Not Deepu's fault)	and she becamme.. NINJA NANI	
Then Nani was mean to Deepu (HAHAHA)	and her powrs diss dyspnd went away (OH NO!)	And some bad guys kip kyp kidnepd them! (spoon gun)
But then Nani and Deepu beame freinds (sorry / Its ok)	Nani's powerse came bak! (AAA DISHOOM / HELP! MUMMY! / WAH!)	and now... they keep the town safe togethr!

* Read all about it in "Ninja Nani and the Bum-bling Burgers"

Hang on ... Something else you need to see before

One

The Daily Bakbak

Mummy Opens Mummy

By Our Special Correspondent

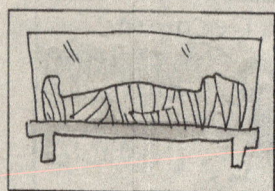

At a special ceremony last evening, the Gadbadnagar Museum formally inaugurated its latest exhibit- the town's very own mummy. Dating back to the time of Chandragupta Maurya, the mummy was discovered two months ago in the municipal landfill, where all the town's garbage is deposited daily. The mummy was found in an underground cavern after the driver of a dumper truck accidentally drove his vehicle into a deep ditch while watching a video on his mobile phone. 'It was not my fault,' he said, when questioned. 'The video had a singing toilet seat in it.'

In a special touch, the Mauryan mummy was inaugurated by the Mayor's own mother. 'The mummy looks like my Uncle Champak,' she said to reporters later. When told that the mummy was wrapped in bandages, she explained that Uncle Champak had been wrapped in bandages too, after a skiing mishap in Auli. 'He'd been trying to take a selfie,' she said.

'Let us hope the mummy will increase interest in the museum,' the Mayor said, as he ate the tiffin his mummy had packed for him. 'The Mauryan Mummy is actually a daddy,' **Mr. Aflatoon Pocha, Director of Gadbadnagar Museum**, joked, when interviewed later. The Mayor was not amused.

Detailed report pg 11

SHHHH! Be patient ... Just one more thing before you read
One

And since we are talking of superpowers ...

ZIP!

Fast as a flash, faster than lightning, Ninja Deepu leaps over mountains, sails over seas, to reach his master, the all-powerful Ninja Dragon Morimori.

'I knew you would come,' Morimori says.

'I will never fail you, Master,' Ninja Deepu replies.

Together, they move through the five battle stances, preparing for battle.

ZAP!

'Stop jumping on the sofa, Deepu!' Daddy says.

'Turn that TV down,' Mummy says.

Deepu's fists clenched.

His eyes narrowed.

His hair stood on end—actually, his hair always stood on end, since he could never remember to comb it. Then ...

ZAPOW!

He shrugged, lowered the volume of the TV and settled down to watch his favourite *Ninja Dragon Morimori*. It was a re-run, but the episode was one he really liked—where the Ninja Dragon confronts the Crooked Grasshopper, evil general of the Jade Army, defeats her in battle and frees the poor villagers she has forced into slavery.

'HEEHEEHHEEE!' the warlord sniggered, swishing her sword about. 'You cannot win against me, Morimori!'

And in a flash of light, she disappeared.

'Dark magic!' Morimori exclaimed. 'Grasshopper, show yourself!'

Another flash of light! This time, a hundred warlords appeared, each an identical copy of the Grasshopper, and each swishing a gleaming sword and laughing.

Morimori's eyes narrowed. He tightened his grip on his sword as the hundred Grasshoppers encircled him and began closing in. He muttered a quick spell.

'You called?' A bird fluttered down to his shoulder.

Morimori had the power to talk to birds and animals. Deepu laughed as the bird, which could see through the Grasshopper's spell, helped the Ninja Dragon by marking the real warlord.

'EWWW!' the warlord squealed, as the bird's droppings landed on her head. Fast as a flash, faster than lightning, the Ninja Dragon had dashed her sword from her hand. PUFF! In an instant, the ninety-nine other Grasshoppers vanished.

Deepu's Nani was slowly acquiring the Ninja Dragon's powers too, though they seemed to appear rather randomly in Nani. Luckily for her, she had the Ninja Dragon's greatest fan on hand for help.

The defeated Grasshopper ran, squealing. Morimori turned to thank his little feathered friend.

As the credits rolled, Deepu wondered if Nani had acquired the power to talk to birds and animals yet.

All right, stop complaining! Here is
One

It was the day of Class IV-C's annual class trip. The children filed glumly out of the bus. You'd think the children would have been a teensy bit more excited, wouldn't you? A whole day away from school, a day without grumpy class teachers, boring lessons, surprise class tests and the prospect of homework, right?

Yeah, right.

IV-A was at the new aquarium, full of exotic fish and touchscreen display screens. IV-B, Deepu's best friend Zeeshan's class, was visiting a butterfly park. And IV-C ...

'Ugh! A whole day at the museum!' Anmol groaned, slapping a hand to his forehead. It made a loud, clanging noise; he'd forgotten he was holding his tiffin box. But even that wasn't enough to cheer up his classmates.

'Come on, line up, children,' Mr Thakchuke, their maths teacher mumbled, in a voice he himself could barely hear. He was accompanying them because Ms Coutinho, their class teacher, had fallen down a manhole on a busy street while texting her best friend. Fortunately, a great pile of wet garbage had broken her fall. Unfortunately, it also swallowed her phone. It took four hours before someone on the street above unplugged their earphones and looked away from *their* phones long enough to hear her shrill cries for help.

Deepu stood with his friends, excited but also a little worried. Mummy was the Chief Curator at the museum, in charge of organising all the exhibits. Deepu often dropped by the old building after school, and spent hours wandering through its enormous rooms, peering into dusty exhibit cases and rickety cabinets.

But coming here with his class was another thing altogether. It meant listening to Vedant sneering at everything; it meant Meera spouting facts like a studious—and very annoying—volcano and Akshay pointing out cracks in the glass and dust on the exhibits. And worst of all, it meant the prospect of Mummy joining them and giving them a personal tour of her favourite exhibits.

'Form a queue,' a man in a spotless white shirt announced. He stood well away from the children, as if he didn't want any of them brushing against him. He flashed a weak smile at the class, but they were too busy gaping at the neat little tower of curls he'd fashioned his hair into.

'Like that tower, no? The one that leans? In Pizza,' Anmol said.

'Pisa!' Meera sniffed.

'Or like the hands of a clock,' Bilquis giggled. 'Showing ten minutes past two.'

It was Doraiswami, Mr Pocha's new assistant. Deepu barely knew him; the man went about his business as quietly as a mouse. Even now, it was easy to miss him in the noise and crush of his bored classmates shuffling about the room.

'Isn't Jamshedbhai around? Or Tsering?' Deepu asked, looking for the cheerful guides who usually walked schoolchildren around the museum.

'Ah, hello, Deepu.' The weak smile flashed again. 'Tsering has her college exams.' Doraiswami pulled a little bottle out of his hands and shook it vigorously into his hands. A sharp, sweet smell filled the air. A dry rustling noise followed, as Doraiswami rubbed the sanitiser into his palms. 'And Jamshed,' Doraiswami sighed, 'is on sick leave. He fell over at Gadbadnagar Lake Park this weekend, while trying to take a selfie.'

'That can't be so bad,' Deepu said, thinking of the soft thick grass in the popular picnic spot.

'He was on a camel ride.'

Grown-ups and their phones, Deepu thought, shaking his head sadly. It was a disease—they were like those friends of his who had turned into zombies from going to tuition class[1].

Doraiswami led the children through the Main Hall, a sprawling room filled with an assortment of exhibits in glass-topped tables, cabinets and old frames along the walls. 'Our Gadbadnagar Museum is home to many interesting artefacts. Fossils ...'

'Fake,' Vedant sneered.

'Garments from the time of Tughlaq ...'

'Hah! Ancient chaddis!' Vedant brayed with laughter. A few low sniggers were also heard.

'And the famous Gadbadnagar mummy!' Doraiswami finished, his face scrunched up into a scowl from the effort of enduring Vedant.

'My father said it's seven feet tall and all shrivelled and everything!' Oily Justin said.

'It's not seven fee—' Doraiswami tried to explain.

---

[1] See *Ninja Nani and the Zapped Zombie Kids*

'No, dummy. It's three feet tall. My friend's father's cousin said.' That was Tall Justin, from the back of the line, swaying on his skinny legs like a palm tree in the breeze, almost a foot taller than everyone else in Class IV. 'And it's wrapped in band-aids.'

'Bandages! Not band-aids!' Doraiswami and Meera snapped, at the exact same moment.

'Maybe ith goth fangth and clawth, dwipping blooth and all!' Faizal said. Everybody ducked to avoid the spray from his mouth; he was still struggling with the retainers his dentist had fitted to his teeth the week before.

'What rubbish!' Bilquis said. 'It's a mummy, okay. Not a vampire!'

'Ooh! Vampire!' breathed AnuManu, who were really two girls called Anusha and Manpreet, who did everything together, including speaking.

The children filed slowly past faded photographs of the Ellora Caves, dusty portraits of freedom fighters and a plaster replica of Hammurabi's Code. Someone had stuck a Hello Kitty sticker on it; wordlessly, Doraiswami ripped it off as he passed, then reached for his hand sanitiser again.

'You know how the Egyptians used to make mummies?' Meera announced.

'Yes,' Oily Justin grumbled. 'But you're going to tell us anyway.'

Meera pretended not to hear him. 'They used to take out its heart and kidneys and stuff and put them in jars all separate-separate. And then they'd put a pointy stick up its nose and ...'

'Tcheee! Shut up! I'm eating!' Anmol screeched, half a sandwich hanging out of his mouth.

'You are always eating!' Meera snorted. 'And then ...'

'Shhh,' whispered Mr Thakchuke, smiling and waving his hands at the chattering line of children. As usual, no one heard him.

'And anyway, this mummy is not Egyptian,' Akshay added. 'It's Indian. From the Shaurya period.'

'Not Shaurya, dumbo. Maurya. Like, Chandragupta Maurya.' Meera again, of course. 'And guess where they found it? In the garbage dump outside Gadbadnagar!'

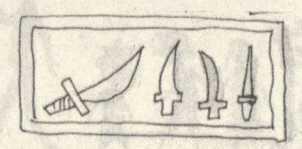

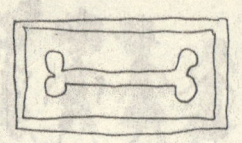

'Haw! Tcheee!' chorused AnuManu.

The children ambled through an arrangement of dusty cases filled with dinosaur bones.

'Maybe it's a fake,' Vedant scoffed, eying Deepu from the corner of his eyes. 'Like these plastic dinosaurs, eh, Deepu?'

'Plaster,' Doraiswami furrowed his brow. 'They are called plaster replicas. They aren't fake.'

Gadbadnagar was only a small town; its museum wasn't considered as important as the ones in the bigger cities, and a lot of the exhibits were copies of real artefacts from the larger museums in the country.

'Maybe ith a thombie!' Faisal suggested, making everyone near him duck again. 'Ith bite will turn everyone into a thombie! Like a ... like a ... ditheath!'

'Eee! Disease!' AnuManu gasped.

'Maybe it's wearing El Toothbrush's chaddis!' Vedant brayed. 'Eh, Deepu?'

'Iltutmish, dodo!' Meera scoffed.

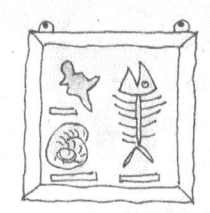

On the class trip to the museum last year, Mummy had personally walked them around an exhibit of garments from the various dynasties of the Delhi Sultanate, and lectured them on the history of every last piece of clothing on display. Iltutmish's underpants had been the highlight of the display.

'And this is the Emperor Shah Jahan!' Doraiswami bellowed, glaring at the noisy children.

Vedant brayed even louder as the children gathered around a statue of the great Mughal, made entirely out of recycled juice cartons and papier mache, by the Gadbadnagar Girls' School's art department. The statue had an arm raised; on it was glued a tiny plastic snow globe with a tinier plastic Taj Mahal in it. Its other hand arm was crooked; one finger seemed to point at Shah Jahan's ear. It was rumoured to have a secret compartment inside it somewhere. Mrs Pocha, who was principal of the Girls' School, had proudly gifted it to the Mayor. The Mayor had taken one look at the cross-eyed statue with its drooping moustache and a dent in its forehead (from being dropped down a flight of stairs while being brought to his office) and promptly donated it to the museum so that the whole town could enjoy it.

Deepu sighed as he stared across the room, at the Rajput exhibit. It seemed to have acquired a new addition since he'd been here last. As if the juice-box Shah Jahan wasn't bad enough! Now here was a second life-size statue, leaning against the wall in the far corner, wearing a coat of chain mail and a helmet. Who knew what they'd recycled to build it?

'And now,' the guide said, leading them across the room, 'the Rajputs.'

KHRAAAAAAROON!

With a chilling roar, the Rajput warrior sprang upright, straight at the children!

Two

It was a good ten minutes before everyone had been shushed, scolded and dragged out from under exhibit tables and behind dusty cabinets, back into the line. Then Doraiswami turned a stern eye on the warrior.

'Mr Chitnis!' he scolded, glaring at the old man who stood blinking at them from behind a pair of thick spectacles. 'You cannot hide in the museum and scare the children!'

'Tcha! I wasn't scaring them!' Mr Chitnis exclaimed, waving a dismissive hand at the children huddled behind Doraiswami. 'I was just trying on the armour here, and got tired. I must have nodded off for a second, that's all!'

The children stared at the ninety-three-year old man before them, covered in rusty old armour with an enormous helmet wobbling and jangling on his head. He stared back at them, his eyes huge behind his thick glasses, his mouth largely free of teeth.

'Buth you screameth ath uth!' Faizal complained.

Mr Chitnis ducked, then replied, 'Nonsense! I was only yawning!'

'You cannot sleep here! And you definitely cannot try on our exhibits!' Doraiswami scolded.

Mr Chitnis made a face as the young man bustled about, stripping the armour and helmet off the old man, until he stood there in his rumpled kurta-pajama and monkey cap.

The children stood around, chattering and giggling nervously and trying not to trip over Vedant who had fainted when the 'statue' came to life, and now lay sprawled across Mr Thakchuke's large feet.

When Vedant had finally been revived and laughed at, the group continued.

'And now for the Marathas!' Doraiswami said tiredly.

'Sir, sir, mummy, sir!' Bilquis whined, tugging on the guide's hand.

'Yes, sir, pleeeeease!' Everyone else joined in, even Mr Thakchuke.

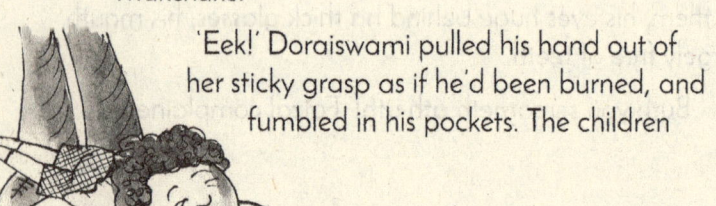

'Eek!' Doraiswami pulled his hand out of her sticky grasp as if he'd been burned, and fumbled in his pockets. The children tittered as he fished out his sanitiser again.

'Time is now 3.15,' Biliquis quipped, pointing at Doraiswami's hair; the hairy tower on his head had collapsed further.

'All right! Come on!' Doraiswami led them up a flight of stairs and down a corridor, and finally waved a hand at the doorway of another large room. 'This is the Gadbadnagar mummy!'

'Ooooh!' everyone said.

Faizal gasped. 'What if the mummy attackth uth? What if it twieth to eat uth?'

'Hai! Eath uth ... I mean, eat us!' AnuManu's mouths widened in identical Os.

'Like-like a thombie!' Faizal added, watching AnuManu closely.

'Hoo! Thombieth!'

The children stared at one another for a moment.

Then, as one, they screamed, 'Awesome!' Jostling each other, they hurried forward to the large dais in the middle of the room.

Thick ropes cordoned the children off from the dais, on which a low platform stood. And on it, in a large glass box lay—the mummy.

It was very, very old.

It lay, swathed in yellowed strips of cloth, lit by a series of lights placed around the glass case.

It was ...

It was ...

'Uff! Boring!' AnuManu sulked, as the children trooped sadly down the stairs.

'That,' Doraiswami said icily, 'was a piece of Gadbadnagar's history. It is very old.'

'Vethy old and vethy bothing,' Faizal declared, forgetting all fears of being eaten.

Doraiswami, who hadn't ducked, flinched and hurried out of Faizal's reach, his hands reaching into his pockets.

'All covered it was. I couldn't see it, even,' Oily Justin whined.

'Or its claws, all covered in blood and all!' Anmol said, through a mouthful of cheese puffs.

Their guide made a choking noise, still wiping his face.

'It was so small,' sneered Vedant. 'Like Deepu.' A few children giggled.

'It was lying flat, just like you, Vedant!' Meera said loudly. That got far more giggles.

'I-I tripped, okay!' Vedant stammered, slinking away.

'That mummy didn't get up or anything!'

'Didn't even moan.'

'Or try to eath uth,' AnuManu complained, as the class trooped down a corridor towards Mr Pocha's office. Faizal frowned at them but said nothing.

'Must be fake, like the dinosaurs,' Vedant mumbled, but no one seemed to hear him.

Ahead of the line, Deepu saw Doraiswami stop and stare at the children for a moment, then swivel around and march towards the exit. Just as he disappeared from view, Deepu saw him pull his phone out of his pocket and start chattering into it.

He shook his head again. Grown-ups and their phones, he thought. Most definitely a disease. Or as Faizal would say, a ditheath.

'Hello!' boomed a cheery voice. It was Mr Pocha, the jovial Director of the Museum. 'Had fun?' He waved to the children as they trooped by his office.

Deepu stopped to smile and wave back. He liked Mr Pocha, who was kind and funny and seemed to enjoy wandering through the old museum building by himself almost as much as Deepu did.

'Yoohoo!' It was Mummy, dressed in one of her blindingly colourful kurtas, hurrying towards them. 'Did you see the Delhi Sultanate garment exhibit? Especially the Iltutmish section? I could take you ...'

'Bye!' Deepu hurried away, behind his class.

Meanwhile, in the space between
Two and Three ...

SOMEONE IS WATCHING OVER GADBADNAGAR AS IT SLEEPS.

HER NINJA SENSES TUNE INTO THE QUIET HUM OF THE NIGHT AIR, BREATHING AND SIGHING AND SNORING IN TUNE WITH THE TOWN'S SLEEPING RESIDENTS.

THE TOWN'S BURGLARS AND VANDALS SEEM TO HAVE TAKEN A BREAK TONIGHT, ITS MANY PUPPIES AND KITTENS AND FLEDGLINGS ARE STAYING CLOSE TO THEIR MOMMIES AND FAR FROM DANGER.

PERHAPS IT'S TIME TO GO HOME, NANI THINKS.

YAAAAWN!

BOING! BOING! BOING!

SUDDENLY...

CLICK! CLICK! CLICK! CLICK! ??! CLICK! CLICK! CLICK! CLICK!

HEY, MYSTERY HERO! SAY **CHEESE!**

Nani freezes for an instant, then cartwheels—
HIYAAA! —sideways and disappears in the shadows.

A young man with a camera runs after her, clicking wildly. 'Get moving, Aftab!' he calls. 'The Mystery Hero is getting away!'

A skinny teenager rolls up on a bright orange scooter, steadying it with his feet. 'Changez bhai, Ammi said not to take her scooter out at night.' The boy's face is almost completely obscured by a wobbly helmet, also orange, with the word 'SuperAmmi' painted in white and black across the back.

'Arrey, this is breaking news! You'll be famous, Affu! A news reporter, just like me!' The man with the camera throws himself onto the back of the scooter, causing it to shake wildly.

'But you aren't a reporter, bhai. You serve tea in the canteen of the newspaper office!'

'Start driving!'

With one final wobble, the scooter takes off, in pursuit of Nani.

Three

Papa gasped, 'The Mystery Hero to be unmasked!'

'What! Where!' Deepu cried.

'It says so right here!' Papa said, reading out the headlines from the Saturday edition of the *Gadbad Gazette*. 'Someone called Changez Baingani has written to the newspaper claiming he will unveil the Hero's identity soon! He says the Hero is just an actor in a superhero costume!'

'What about all the people the Hero's helped? The burglars he caught?' Deepu cried.

'He says they are all actors too!' Papa read out. 'He says he's going to prove it very soon!'

Deepu glared at the paper. The Mystery Hero was no fake! *She* was a living, breathing ninja. In fact, she was right there at the table with them—his very own Nani! Her ninja senses would have told her if the boy, or anyone else in Gadbadnagar was in danger! He swung around, just in time to see her ...

YAAAAWN

Nani's eyelids drooped. She was dozing—at breakfast! Poor Nani, Deepu thought. Being a secret superhero was really taking a toll on her—all the nights out catching villains, rescuing people caught in burning buildings and even the odd cat stuck in a tree, were leaving her quite exhausted.

A sparrow landed on the window sill and trilled loudly. Nani turned sharply, and started. She stared at the bird, and then at Deepu. 'It's ... it's talking to me!' she whispered.

Deepu grinned and nodded. 'About time!' he whispered.

Nani smiled as the bird chirped again, then flew away. 'She says I rescued her babies last night,' Nani whispered. 'They'd fallen out of their nest. She came to say thank you.'

'Personally,' Papa mused, still engrossed in his paper, 'I think he's real. Gadbadnagar's very own superhero!' His eyes shone through his glasses as he imagined a caped hero flying over the town. Deepu stifled a grin. If only Papa knew his hero was three feet away, in a frilly pink housecoat and furry bunny slippers, making faces at him over her oatmeal. Still reading, Papa reached across the table for a paratha.

Nani flicked her wrist and mumbled a few words. A napkin glided across the table, straight into Papa's hand. Deepu watched as Papa raised the napkin to his mouth and, still reading, began chewing on it. After a few moments, he frowned. Then, still reading, he dipped the napkin into his coffee and began chewing it again.

AAAAAAAAAAAAAAAA!

A scream ripped through the house.

Deepu's paratha flew out of his fingers and landed—PLOP!—in Papa's coffee. Papa almost swallowed the napkin in his hand.

Mummy rushed into the room.

> THE MUMMY'S ATTACKED SOMEONE!

Four

Papa looked sternly at Nani. 'Really, Ma,' he said. 'You need to be nice to the neighbours.'

'Not *my* mummy, Rajiv!' Mummy snapped. '*The* mummy! The one in the museum! I've just had a call from Mr Pocha!'

Papa ducked back into the safety of the sports page. Mummy took a deep breath, put her hands on her hips and sang,

HOOLOOLOOLOOLOO...

'Another of your stress-busting techniques, Priya?' Nani asked, when it was safe to remove her fingers from her ears.

'Yes, Ma.' Mummy sighed. 'And it's not helping.' She took another deep breath.

'Here, eat something, dear,' Papa said hurriedly, offering her his napkin.

Mummy groaned and collapsed into a chair. 'Mr Pocha's been up half the night with the police, poor man!' she said. 'He says he got a call from one of the security guards at one in the morning, claiming the mummy had come alive and tried to eat her in the ladies' washroom! They've had to send her to the hospital!'

'Send whom?' Nanny asked. 'The mummy? Did eating the guard upset its stomach?'

'I thought the mummy was a daddy,' Papa observed.

'Very funny, both of you. The guard is in the hospital. She was unharmed, thankfully, but in a state of shock.'

'Is the Gadbadnagar mummy really running loose in the museum?'

'It can't be! It's ... dead! And it's locked up in its glass case, just like it was last night. The locks on the room are untouched too—Mr Pocha checked. Even the security cameras show no one coming or going from that room.'

'So who tried to eat the guard?'

'Maybe she met Mr Chitnis,' Papa observed. 'He does seem to keep falling asleep in there.'

Mummy rolled her eyes. 'He spends more time at the museum than I do. But no, the guard was insistent it was the mummy. Not Mr Chitnis.'

'You should just keep him on as an exhibit,' Papa joked. 'The Living Mummy—no, Daddy—no, Grandaddy! Hehehe!'

Deepu sat there, half-listening as the rest of his family talked.

A real, live people-eating monster!

Right here in Gadbadnagar!

Right where Mummy worked!

'Awesome!' he whispered to himself.

You'd think a nine—nearly ten—year-old boy would know better than to believe in silly things like monsters, right? Then again, if you had seen your TV turn your granny into a superhero[2], and you had been turned into a zombie by an evil creature that hopped out of the TV set[3], you might believe in people-munching monsters too.

'I'm going to have to go to work today,' Mummy sighed. 'The police have been called. My first free Saturday in months, ruined by a mummy!'

---

[2] See *Ninja Nani and the Bumbling Burglars*
[3] See *Ninja Nani and the Zapped Zombie Kids*

Deepu thought about all the Saturdays—and Sundays—he'd spent in chess camps, abacus classes and maths tutorial sessions, all because of *his* mummy, but wisely said nothing.

Mummy buried her head in her hands. 'And all this just as we are about to unveil the new exhibit!' she wailed. 'It could have finally brought people back to the museum, revived their interest in history.'

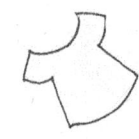

'That's what you said about the chaddi-banian exhibit last year,' Nani said.

'Uff! Please, Ma. It was an exhibition of commonly used garments from the time of Tughlaq. It was a refreshing peek into lesser-known aspects of history, into the everyday lives of common people.'

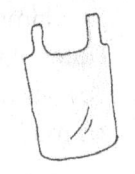

'So what's the new exhibit about, dear?' Papa asked.

'Backscratchers from the Second Battle of Panipat,' Mummy said.

Nani snorted. Papa hid behind his paper.

'Ma, those were essential accessories for every soldier who went to battle!' Mummy said. 'You try wearing a heavy coat of armour on a hot battlefield for twelve hours straight! I tell you, those backscratchers saved lives!'

'On a battlefield?'

'Hmmphh! My point is, history isn't just the important dates, it's the small, everyday details too. The cups and spoons and, yes, underwear and backscratchers all played as much a part in making history as the Taj Mahal!'

'You should print that on a t-shirt, Priya,' Papa smiled, as he and Deepu started clearing the table.

'Or on chaddis,' Nani said. 'They would sell like hotcakes in the museum gift shop.'

Mummy took another deep breath. Papa, Deepu and Nani reached for their ears.

Meanwhile, in the early hours, before
Five

Two in the morning. Everyone in Gadbadnagar is asleep ...

BOING! BOING! BOING! Nani backflips across the park, swings through the trees, cartwheels past the rock garden!

HAI! HUP! HIYAAA! Nani practices the five battle stances!

She straightens up, thinking of the thief she caught in an electronics store earlier in the night, the teenage boys about to spray rude words on the wall of the Gadbadnagar Shopping Centre, the puppies that had strayed away from their mother.

SWOOOOSH! She leaps across the old pond, landing lightly on her feet.

The boys have been scolded and sent home, the thief tied up and left for the police to find, and the puppies safely back with their mother.

Time to go home, she thinks. Is Gadbadnagar safe for the night?

Her question is answered by a very faint 'HELP!'

Strange, Nani thinks, even as she runs into the park. No jingling.

You know about the jingling, don't you? The noise Nani hears whenever her ninja senses detect someone in trouble? If you have any Santa Claus jokes to share, this is NOT the time and place, thank you.

'HELP! PLEASE HELP!' The cry is louder.

Nani stops, surveys her surroundings, zooms ahead. Not Hawaldar Tambe, I hope, she thinks. He's always blowing on his whistle and then getting chased up a tree by that grumpy little Pongo.

You do know about Pongo, don't you? The pug, also called the Son of Satan, who lives at Pammi Aunty's, next door to Deepu and likes nothing better than chasing people up trees to show them who's boss.

But no, this isn't Mr Chitnis. And it isn't the whistling hawaldar either.

Err, help me, Mystery Hero!
Seriously? That branch...
...barely weighs anything!
SWIP!!
....
DID YOU SAY 'SORRY'? WHY?
ERR, FOR WHAT'S GOING TO HAPPEN NEXT.
CLICK!
CLICK!
CLICK!
HUH? WHAT'S GOING TO HAP..OH!
CLICK!
CLICK!
MYSTERY HERO! SAY CHEEEESE!
CLICK!
CLICK!
CLICK!

Something small and feathered lands on her shoulder. 'It's the humans I saw at the old well yesterday!' The sparrow twitters in her ear. 'They've been here all night! Kept my babies awake with their loud chattering!!'

The man with the camera runs about under the tree, still yelling. 'Come out, Mystery Hero! I just want a photo!' He runs around, looking for Nani, before finally heaving to a stop under the tree. 'Tcha! Missed him again!' he grunts.

'Changez bhai, I'm tired!' The boy whines. 'I want to go home!'

'Be quiet, Altaf!' The man snaps. 'I told you to act like you were hurt so the Hero would be fooled! Useless you ... Agh! Horrid bird!' He wipes a great blob of bird poop off his head. 'Now, where is that Hero?'

Five

'Long day, Priya?' Papa looked up from his laptop, as Mummy came in from work the following evening.

'Half of Gadbadnagar turned up at the museum today!' Mummy sighed, dropping down into a chair.

'For your backbiters exhibit?' asked Papa.

'Backscratchers, Rajiv!' Mummy said. 'And no, they came to see the mummy! Great crowds of them, all clamouring to see the "Monster Mummy" stagger around and eat someone! People queued up for hours to get in!

'Isn't that what you've always wanted, dear?' Papa asked, handing her a cup of tea.

'Yes,' Mummy groaned. 'And it was terrible! The crowds! The noise! All those people taking selfies with the mummy! What was I thinking!'

She turned on the TV.

'The Mystery Hero revealed!' screamed the news.

Everyone's eyes swiveled towards the TV. 'First the paper, now the TV!' Papa scoffed. 'That fellow moves fast!'

On the screen, Changez was trying to look very important, as he talked to a reporter. 'Yes,' he said. 'My good name Changez Baingani! I want to say Mystery Hero is a fake, a phoney number one!'

Even the reporter looked startled. 'Why?' she asked.

'The Mystery Hero refused to save my innocent little brother, who was trapped under a fallen tree. I have pictures to prove it!'

The reporter looked the photographs Changez held up. 'Those are pictures of trees. And someone's foot.'

Changez blushed. 'Err, yes, the Hero got away this time.'

'That man!' Nani hissed. 'I met him last night!'

The camera swiveled around onto the thin, pimply face of the boy Nani had found under a branch. His head and right arm seemed wrapped in bandages. Nani frowned; he certainly hadn't been injured last night.

'Myself Altaf,' the teenager stuttered into the mic, staring at the camera with wide eyes. 'Myself, er, innocent. Means, I was ... just walking, like, and suddenly, like, this huge tree, like, fell on me, and, like, whatever.' He raised his bandaged arm and scratched his forehead vigorously.

Changez swatted the boy's arm down. 'And you were trapped and badly injured, weren't you?'

'Uhh, yes, yes.' The boy blushed. He raised his bandaged arm again, and began chewing his fingernails. Again, Changez swatted it down.

'And did the Mystery Hero come and save you?'

'Yes!' The boy said, then turned the colour of a ripe tomato as he looked at Changez. 'Means, like, no! No! Definitely!' Then he gulped and looked down at his toes.

'See!' Changez said triumphantly. 'The Hero's a fake! A phoney! I'll prove it!'

Deepu fumed. How dare they! All Nani did was help! They didn't even know *she* was their Hero, not some stupid man in tights and a tablecloth around his neck! Yet all they did was sneer and make fun of her—like Vedant at school.

'It was a trap!' Nani said in a low voice.

'What?' Deepu whirled around.

'For the Mystery Hero,' Nani continued. 'They wanted to take photographs of her! The boy was just pretending to be trapped!'

Mummy switched off the TV.

'Maybe the Mystery Hero should come visit your mummy,' Papa joked.

'Eh?' Mummy and Nani said.

'Not ... umm, your mummy, dear,' Papa said. 'Your haunted mummy! At the museum! The mummy that is actually a daddy, hehehe!'

'It is not haunted, Rajiv!' Mummy replied. 'Or cursed. It's just a mummy. In a glass box. It cannot possibly be roaming around, snacking on people!'

'I'm sure all this excitement will die away in a couple of days, Priya,' Nani said. 'It'll turn out to be a prank.'

'Or Mr Chitnis in Tughlaq's dressing gown!' Papa chipped in.

Some things you absolutely must see before
Six

Mummy returns... and curses!
Mysterious messages left on museum walls; police clueless

Mummy from Mars!
Old Age Home resident claims mummy is an alien!

Mummy steals Tughlak's undies!
Artefacts missing from museum: Is the mummy a thief?

Mummy opens match
Mayor's mummy inaugurates inter school kho kho tournament

First undies stolen, now backscratchers: is the mummy itchy?

Mummies beat daddies ..again!
Sole womens' team retains trophy at Gadbadnagar Parents' Association's annual kabaddi meet

Six

The news had spread like wildfire across the school. Everyone in Class IV seemed to have collected around Deepu's desk in the short break.

'Is it true? The mummy's roaming the museum eating everyone?'

'And thealing thuff!' That was Faizal; everyone ducked.

'Ooh! Thealing thuff!' AnuManu squealed.

'Does it really leave messages on the wall?'

'How come it writes in English? Did they know English in the Shaurya period?'

'Maurya, you dodo! Maurya!'

'Chaddis!' Vedant sniggered. 'It took El Toothbrush's chaddis!'

'Aaargh! Iltutmish!' Meera looked like she was about to explode.

Deepu felt his face redden. It was true; things had gone missing at the museum. Iltutmish's underpants were missing from their display case along with several other exhibits from the Mamluk dynasty display. And last night, some Rajput backscratchers had been taken.

'It's probably itchy under all those band-aids,' Tall Justin remarked. 'But why does it need chaddis?'

'Bandages!' Meera snapped. 'And it's not itchy—it's haunted! It wants revenge! Or maybe, a sacrifice!' She rubbed her hands in glee. Her puff of hair waggled in the air as she spoke. AnuManu looked at the excitement in her face and took a cautious step backwards.

'My mother says those things from the museum are very valuable,' Deepu said. 'There are collectors around the world who would pay a lot of money for artefacts like that.'

'For backscratchers? And gigantic yellow underpants?' Anmol asked, halfway through a paratha. Everyone ducked again.

'Uh-huh.'

'But why would the mummy need money?'

'And how come the watchmen have not caught it?'

The night watchmen had fled the museum almost immediately after news of the mummy had broken. Doraiswami had arranged for a private security firm to patrol the museum, but none of the men or women sent to keep guard outside the mummy's room had seen a thing. In desperation, Mr Pocha had had extra security cameras installed all over the museum, operated by secret codes known only to himself and his assistant. But strangely, they seemed to switch themselves off every night and then switch back on in the morning.

'How come the Mythery Hero hathn't caught it?'

'Aah! Mythery Hero!' AnuManu fell over, giggling.

'You're right!' The rest of the children pitched in. 'How come?'

Deepu pressed his pencil so hard into his notebook, the point snapped and flew across the room. Nani would have solved this by now, if it hadn't been for that awful Changez Baingani. He seemed to turn up everywhere with his silly assistant and his camera. Nani could barely leave the house anymore without him popping up from behind a bush or from inside a manhole, screeching, 'Say cheese!'

'I heard the museum's been closed!' Bilquis said.

'Closed to the public,' Deepu explained. 'No one is allowed in, except people who work there!'

'I think,' Meera said, 'we should go to the museum and ...'

'And what? Get eaten?' Vedant scoffed.

'Eaten!' gasped AnuManu.

'No! Catch the mummy in action!' Meera said. 'With a camera! Like that Changez Baingani on the news!'

'Mad or what? Then you'll be the one covered in band-aids!'

'Ooh! Band-aids!'

'Bandages! Bandages! It's wearing ban—'

Deepu half-listened as his classmates continued chattering and squabbling around him. Of course! Someone had to sneak into the museum, someone brave and strong and clever, who wouldn't be afraid of a withered three-hundred-year-old man in band-aids. Someone people assumed was small and weak, but was really very different inside. And that person wasn't Meera, or Changez, was it? It was ...

Seven

Pongo hid in the bushes by Pammi Aunty's front gate, listening.

Something was up—he could smell it!

All kinds of trouble seemed to be finding its way to Gadbadnagar these days. And that old lady from next door was often in the middle of it. He knew—he had followed her often enough as she swung through the trees and back flipped across the Municipal Park. Pongo knew better than to challenge someone that powerful, so he just lurked in the shadows, watching. And waiting.

CRUNCH! What was that? Pongo's ears pricked up. Someone was creeping along the pavement, someone trying very hard not to make a sound. He rose, a growl rumbling in his throat ... then stopped, listening hard.

Footsteps pattered down the street, hushed whispering followed. Then, more footsteps, more whispers. Something was going on, something smelling of trouble—five kinds of trouble.

ANMOL, BROUGHT A TORCH OR WHAT?
Ya, Meera. On my phone only. Means, my grandpa's phone. But he sleeps by nine, so he won't notice.
CHOMP CHOMP
UFF! YOU BROUGHT TIFFIN! NEVER MIND.. BROUGHT A CAMERA?
Ya Meera. On my phone only.
GREAT. GOT YOUR PHONE?
Err...umm... ... here it is!
I'm thcared! What if ith attackth uth!
Hee! Attackth uth!
Thop ith! Don't theath me! I can'th help thpeaking like thith!
Hoo! Thpeaking like thith!
SSH! STOP FIGHTING!
CHOMP CHOMP

Pongo made a low, growling noise. Then he made a different kind of noise. A terrible smell followed. Well, think of the worst smell you've ever sniffed. How bad would it be on a scale of one to ten? Ooh, that bad, huh? Well, take that score and double it. Now multiply that number by a thousand. Now divide that by eight. Now, hold your nose with one hand, hold your right foot with the other, hop in a circle and repeat:

I'VE JUST BEEN PRANKED.

What, you asked for that! But anyway, where were we?

BLAAARP!

'Oooh!' Meera squeaked, grabbing her nose. 'Tchee, Anmol!'

'What? No! Must be Faizal!'

'Whath? No! Muth be AnuManu!'

'Wha–'

'Shhh!' Meera took charge again. 'Now, where's that Vedant? He said he'd come.'

'Probably too thcared!'

'Hah! Thcared!'

'Probably fainted and lying flat somewhere!'

There were only giggles for a while, then footsteps shuffled away.

But what's this? A hissing! A slithering! A sound like something about to make a great deal of trouble!

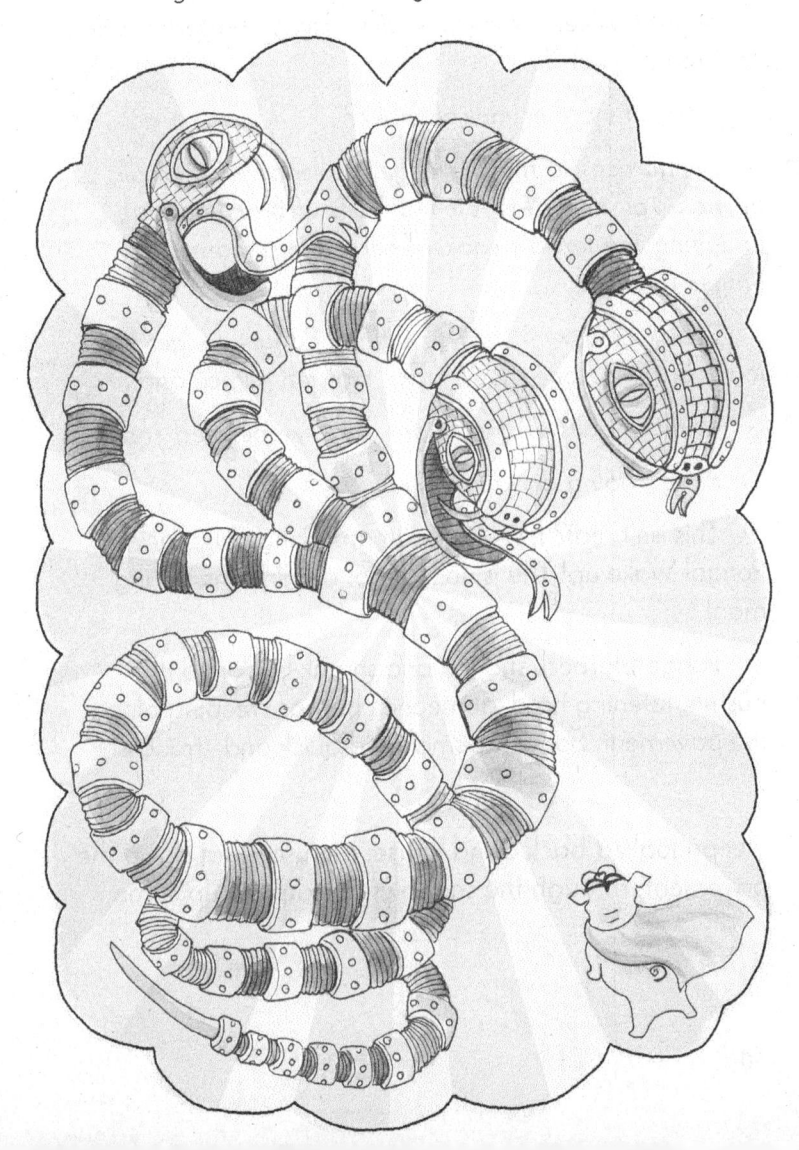

An enormous serpent with one, two—make that three—heads waits on the pavement! Its red eyes glitter, its tongues flicker, its metal scales click, its batteries whirr as it rears up and ...

Wait, it's a mechanical snake?

Pongo rises to the challenge! He leaps into the air, his paws of steel outstretched! Bolts of fire shoot out, engulfing the terrible snake! The snake screams and lunges forward.

Quick as a wink, fast as a flash, Pongo dodges its jaws, backflips one, two—make that ten—times and ...

Wait ... bolts of fire? Giant battery-operated snakes?

Pongo doing backflips?

This isn't real? It's ... it's a dream! Pongo? Pongo? Pongo! Wake up! This is no time for daydreams, young man!

Pongo blarped, snarled and shrank back into the bushes, listening hard. Someone else was creeping along the pavement. Someone small and quick and—trouble!

Deepu looked back at his house, then scuttled down the pavement, through the shadows. He'd piled up some

50

pillows under his quilt to look like he was still sleeping. He knew Nani would never approve of him sneaking into the museum at night. So what if he was nine—nearly ten—years old? Hadn't he stepped up to help his friends when they'd been turned into zombies by the evil Green Gecko? Even Nani had told him he'd been incredibly brave—after she'd scolded him for being reckless. If he could do that for Zeeshan and the rest of his friends, he certainly would for Mummy. And the mummy. Which was really Mummy's mummy. But wait, Mummy's mummy was really Nani ...

Focus, he said sternly to his brain. Then, taking a deep breath, he stepped out of the shadows and ...

. . . was promptly eaten by zombies.

WHAT?! AGAIN??

Just kidding.

No, he was NOT promptly eaten by zombies.

Hey, we aren't even in this story!

Or Pongo.

Or a mummy.

HUH?

Oops. I meant this mummy.

GRRRRAAAARGH!

Nope. Nyet. Nu-uh.

Deepu stepped out of the shadows and ran, as fast as his legs could carry him, towards the museum.

Pongo watched Deepu scamper away down the street. That boy, the pug thought. As much trouble as his granny! Pongo rose up onto his stubby feet to follow Deepu and ...

More footsteps! More scuttling! What was going on in Gadbadnagar tonight? Whatever it was, Pongo was going to sniff it out! Sniff it out and nip it in the ankles, for sure! He snarled silently, crouched, waited, err, blarped ... and watched.

Eight

Deepu crawled through the ventilator and dropped down silently, to the floor below. He was in the basement of the museum, a large dusty room filled with old packing cases, files and broken furniture. He waited for his eyes to get used to the dark, then made his way slowly towards the door.

CRACK!

Deepu froze in his tracks.

A cold chill ran down Deepu's spine. Goosebumps erupted along his arms! There was someone in the room with him. *Someone right behind him...*

Slowly, willing himself not to scream, Deepu turned and ...

.... stared at the person wriggling, like a very itchy snake, in the window.

'Vedant?' he hissed. 'What are you doing here?'

'Help me, na!' Vedant said. 'I'm stuck!'

And indeed he was, with the latch of the window hooked firmly into the seat of his shorts. For an instant, Deepu considered leaving his classmate where he was, then stepped forward and pulled him loose.

'Good thing you are so small,' Vedant smirked, dropping down to the floor without so much as a thank you. 'You can fit easily through these tiny windows!'

'Why are you here, Vedant?' Deepu whispered, ignoring the jibe.

'Meera dared me,' Vedant said. 'I had to come!'

'Is she here too?'

'I bet she was too scared, hah!'

Deepu said nothing, but turned towards the door and froze!

'Did you hear that?' he asked. 'Like whispering?'

'Don't leave me here!' Vedant wailed at once, clutching at Deepu.

'Shhhh!' Deepu shook free of Vedant's clammy hands. 'Listen!'

'Okay,' Vedant said and promptly sneezed.

'Shhh!'

'I have dust allergies!'

'Okay, now be qui–'

Deepu sighed. He waited another minute, but the building was silent. He tiptoed to the door and peered out into the corridor. It was quiet and dark, lit only by the dim streetlight filtering in through the window at the far end.

'Come on–and don't snee–'

'Sorry!'

The boys tiptoed out. Behind them, a dark shadow dropped in through the ventilator ...

Meanwhile, not too far away ...
Changez bhaiya, I'm scared!
You're perfectly safe! Stop moaning!
But I have college tomorrow morning! Ammi will scold me if I don't get up on time!
Altaf, you're such a baby!
I'm not a baby, okay! I'm eighteen!
Yeah, right! Eighteen months! Now, be quiet!
Don't be mean!
I said BE QUIET!!
Just wait till I tell Ammi! Just wait till she finds out you're making me sneak out with you. ANd steal her scooter! AND lie about every......MMFFFRRRGGG!!
That should keep you quiet! Hmph!
MMFFFGGRRHHHDDDRRR!

MMFFGGGRRRR!

Look, I just want to get that Hero fellow here. Then I promise I'll let you down, all right?

I've been chasing the Mystery Hero for days and still don't have a single good photograph of him.! Not one!

And now that reporter has banned me from the TV studio until I get enough proof of the Hero's identity!

So it's time we set a new trap for the Hero..one he can't run away from!

HEHEHEHEHEHEH!

NNGGGRRHHHMMM!

I have a feeling today's my lucky day!

Deepu and Vedant crouched in the dark corridor, just inside the entrance to the garment exhibit room, listening.

CRASH! BIFF! 'MMMFFPPGGGRR!'

Somewhere, in one of the other rooms on the floor, something strange was going on.

'Catch him, Gogi!'

'MMFGGFFF!'

'Bablu! Tie him up, quick!'

'GRNMMMNNGGG!'

'Sounds like a fight,' Vedant whispered.

THUD! BANG! OUCH! 'Mummy! Gogi, he kicked me!'

The boys heard the sound of something heavy being dragged away. The thuds and grunts got fainter, then quietened down.

Deepu flattened himself against the wall, his ear to the doorframe. Who were these people? And what were they doing in the museum this late at night?

'Have they gone?' Vedant said.

'Ssh! They'll hear you!'

'Ya, okay. Have they gone?' Vedant asked again, just as loudly.

'Wait here!' But before Deepu could move, there was a new sound.

TOK! TOK! TOK!

Someone was walking down the corridor, right outside the door they were huddled behind! The footsteps stopped—right outside the door. A shadow fell across the threshold—an enormous shadow that stretched across the floor and melted into the shadows beyond.

Deepu's heart thudded like a drum! Was it the mummy? Had it heard him?

A long moment passed, then another.

'Mummy!' Vedant whimpered. 'I want to go home.' He rubbed his nose and sniffed hard.

Deepu sniffed too. For just a moment, he caught a whiff of something sweet—and familiar. And that other sound, a sort of dry, rustling ...

'Have you sent your men downstairs?' a stern voice said.

'Yes, boss.'

'And is that old man tied up?'

'Yes, boss. In that mummy room. We took his camera too, he was taking pictures of me and my men.'

'Make sure he can't get out.' It was the stern voice again. 'The police have to find him tomorrow.'

'Yes, boss. Heheh, it will look like he stole everything.'

'The truck will be here soon,' the boss continued. 'Make sure you load everything like I told you to. Here's the list.' Paper rustled.

'Old coins. Check. Maratha knives. Check. But ... cooking pots? Backscratchers? Really?'

'They're very valuable.'

'And garments! Old chaddis and banians! Who wants those?'

'You're not being paid to ask questions, Gogi!'

'Yes, boss.'

'Is Elvis patrolling the ground floor?'

'Yes, boss. Wearing full costume also!' Gogi said. 'And we have that horror film soundtrack as well! Very scary!'

Deepu listened to the footsteps get fainter, then peeked out of the doorway.

'One's wearing a uniform like a security guard,' he said to Vedant.

'So what?'

'And the other one, he's—well—wearing some sort of pointy cap.'

'What, like Santa Claus?'

GRAAAOOOOOON!

Deepu was frozen to the ground by the roar that echoed through the building. As the echoes died away, a chorus of other noises started up. Something moaned! Something groaned! Something shuffled! Something shrieked! Something cackled with evil laughter!

Something whined and thudded to the floor near Deepu's feet.

A door creaked shut.

The air filled with horrid whispery ghost voices, hissing and seething into Deepu's ears.

Goosebumps sprang up on Deepu's arms. Icy cold fingers of fear ran up and down his spine.

Then—CLICK! Silence followed, silence so deep and thick you could cut it with a knife.

The only sound Deepu could hear was the violent thudding of his own heart. He waited, too scared to move. The silence continued.

'You can get up now, Vedant,' he said finally to the lump lying across the floor near his feet.

'I-I tripped!' Vedant jumped up to his feet. 'What was that?'

'I don't know,' Deepu frowned.

Deepu waited another minute, his eyes fixed to the doorway. He half-expected something to leap in, but there was no movement.

'I'm going to go look,' he whispered. Vedant did not reply.

'Wait here, okay?' Again, Vedant stayed silent.

Deepu turned. 'Vedant?' he whispered.

Silence—deep, dark silence to match the shadows that had swallowed his classmate. Deepu's arms threw up a new batch of goosebumps; his spine went all chilly and tingly again.

'Vedant, stop fooling around!' More silence.

By day, Deepu had been in this room a hundred times over. He knew every nook and cranny in it, every exhibit and display case. Yet now, in the darkness, the room felt strange and frightening, the shadows filled with scary creatures waiting to grab him. He gulped and took a step forward, then another. 'Vedant?' he whispered again.

A hand reached out of the shadows ...

Nine

And offered him a sandwich.

'Anmol?' Deepu almost choked, staring at the tiffin box thrust under his nose. 'You? Here? And you brought ... tiffin?'

Anmol grinned and kept chewing. Behind him, the bright light of a cellphone torch flared up. A great puff of hair waggled towards them.

'It's Anmol, ya,' Meera said. 'What do you expect?'

'Alwayth eathing thnackth!' Deepu ducked out of habit, as Faizal emerged from a far corner.

'Hah! Eathing thnakth!' AnuManu sniggered from under a display table.

'Thuth up, okay? Don'th be mean!'

'Hee! Thuth up!'

'Did you hear those noises?' Deepu asked.

'Ya, it plays every five minutes or something,' Meera drawled, yawning. 'Like some cheap horror film soundtrack.'

Soundtrack! Hadn't Gogi said something about horror films? Is that what this was?

'Okay, dare done, right?' Vedant peered out from behind a cabinet, looking uneasily into the shadows. 'Can we go now?'

'Why?' Meera sneered. 'Going to faint or what?'

'Listen!' Deepu said hurriedly, before a fight broke out. 'Something's going on here in the museum. We have to leave.'

'We know,' Meera replied. 'We heard those men and came here to hide.'

'Let's go.'

'We'll just see the mummy first.'

'What!' Deepu said. 'No! You can't! You shouldn't! We have to call the police!'

'Relax! I just want a photo with the mum—'

'No! This is no time for selfies!'

'Don't be so bossy, okay?' snapped Meera.

In any other situation, Deepu would have fallen over laughing if she'd said that, since she was the bossiest person, bar none, in Class IV-C. No, in Gadbadnagar. No, on planet earth. Now, however, he just rolled his eyes and let it go.

66

'Ya, tho bothy you are!' Faizal scoffed, then glared at AnuManu. They sniggered but said nothing.

'I'm not bothy—er, bossy! We have to get out!'

Meera glared at him. 'Ya, okay! We'll ... Stop groaning, Vedant.'

'What? I didn't groan! Must be this Faizal.'

'What? Nonthenth! Muth be Anmol.'

'What? Rubbish! I didn't.'

GRAAOOOON!

The children squealed and whirled around.

Something reared up from the shadows and staggered towards them!

It was old!

It was shrivelled!

It was wrapped in lengths of yellowed fabric!

It was ...

'M-Mr Chitnis?' Deepu stammered.

'GRAAAAAAR!'

Mr Chitnis yawned again, then peered at the children through his thick glasses.

'I must have fallen asleep,' he cackled. 'Like this fellow on the floor.'

Everyone looked down and sniggered.

Vedant looked up and blushed. 'I tripped, okay?'

Mr Chitnis adjusted the tattered yellow muffler wrapped around his neck and shoulders. 'Knitted this myself!' he said proudly. 'In 1963, I think. Or was it '64?'

'We have to go. Now!' Deepu said to Meera. 'Come on, I know a way out through the basement.'

Meera peered out of the door. 'We came from the service door near the canteen,' she said. 'It's closer.' Her gaze fell on the door to the mummy exhibit. She grinned. 'Look! They've left the door open!'

'Meera! No!' Deepu cried.

She was off already, tiptoeing towards the mummy. Anmol followed, then AnuManu and Faizal. Vedant stood up hurried after his friends, bleating, 'I really tripped, I swear!'

Mr Chitnis ambled out into the corridor and headed the other way.

Deepu curbed an urge to scream. He had a sudden wish to just leave his foolish classmates to their fate, and escape from the museum. He'd done his best to warn them. Ms Coutinho, the museum guide, Meera—what was it with the people of Gadbadnagar and their phones, he wondered, that made them behave so badly. As for Mr Chitnis, what could a nine—nearly ten—year-old possibly do for a ninety-year-old who insisted on taking naps in dusty museums?

He could tiptoe down to the basement, get out, call the police and tell them about the thieves. And surely Nani's ninja senses would jingle if his friends got into danger. She'd be here in a flash to save them.

Is this what the Ninja Dragon would do, he thought. Is this what Nani would do?

He sighed and darted out of the room.

'Come on, Mr Chitnis. We have to stay together.' Taking the old man's arm firmly, he steered him towards the mummy's room.

Meanwhile, as you ready yourself for the thrill fest that is
Ten

Nani was nearly home, after a night of saving Gadbadnagar—catching thieves, rescuing people stuck in lifts or locked into their toilets, kittens trapped in drains, baby birds that have fallen out of their nests.

ZIP! She raced past the swings in the park.

ZAP! She cartwheeled around the rock garden.

ZAPOW! She backflipped right across the pond.

Something was very wrong.

Nani could feel it. It wasn't just the jingling that grew louder as she ran through the park. There was something else, a worrying feeling that she couldn't quite place. Who could it be?

She ran past some trees, out through the sandpit and swung straight over the fence. She cartwheeled past the Commercial Centre, leapfrogged over the rather ugly fountain in the middle of the roundabout and found herself near the new aquarium.

The jingling grew louder and stronger as she hurried through the parking lot near the aquarium and into the little park beside it.

'You!' Nani frowned as she caught sight of the young boy hanging upside down from a rope looped over a thick tree branch. The boy's eyes widened as he saw her approach.

'Mmmph!' He grunted through the thick tape over his mouth.

'This has gone far enough!' Nani said sternly. 'You and your brother are ...' She shook her head; the jingling just wouldn't go away.

'FFFGGRRRKKKMMNNNN–AIIIII!' Nani ripped the tape off the boy's face.

'What kind of game are you two—'

'RUN!'

'What?' She could barely hear him over the jingling.

'Mystery Hero, run!' The boy screamed. 'RUN!'

Nani whirled around.

SWISH! ZWIP! ZOOOP! Ropes tightened around her, throwing her off her feet, swinging her up into the tree!

And a familiar voice said, 'SAY CH–'

Ten

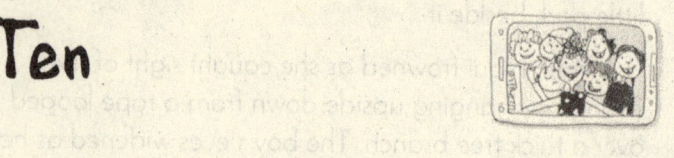

'—EESE!' Meera whispered. **CLICK!**

'Cheese!' 'Cheese!' 'Theeth!'

Everyone crowded together in front of her cellphone. Meera had even fashioned a selfie stick out of a backscratcher and Razia Sultan's favourite handkerchief. The flash went off, blinding everyone for a second. Behind them, looking very small, very old and very dead in its glass case was the Gadbadnagar mummy.

'Right, now we're going!' Deepu said. 'Where's Mr Chitnis?' He sighed. The old man had wandered off again.

'One more, one more,' Meera said, peering down at the picture she'd taken. 'This one is blurred ... Cheese!'

CLICK!

'HYAAANCHOO! Oi, my eyes were shut!'

CLICK!

'Vedant, duffer! Why you pushed me?'

CLICK! CLICK!

'Meera!' Deepu hissed. 'Come on!'

'HYAAANCHOO! Sorry!'

'Ya, wait, I—who's groaning? Vedant?'

'What? No! Must be Faizal!'

'Whath! No! Muth be ...'

GRAOOOOOOOON!

Meera swung around and screamed! The light from the phone flared out across the room, and lit something that reared up from the shadows in the far corner.

Something that moaned and groaned and grew larger by the second as it rose from the shadows in the corner of the room!

The creature was wrapped in lengths of yellowed cloth. It eyes gleamed and glinted from under the bindings.

GRRMMNNGRRRR!

Deepu staggered back against the wall.

Anmol screamed and dove under a table.

Mr Chitnis stood in the far corner, testing a backscratcher on himself.

'It's the mummy!' Meera shrieked. 'It's alive!'

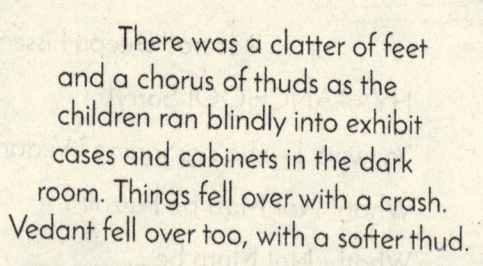

There was a clatter of feet and a chorus of thuds as the children ran blindly into exhibit cases and cabinets in the dark room. Things fell over with a crash. Vedant fell over too, with a softer thud.

'**GRAOOOOON!**' the creature groaned. It seemed to tremble with rage as it fixed its beady eyes on the children.

'**GRAAAAAR!**'

'RUN!' Meera screamed, leaping towards the door. AnuManu and Faizal followed.

The creature seemed to leap into the air and—BOING BOING BOING—hopped after them.

Deepu stared, wide eyed. It was, indeed, bounding forward, like a kangaroo bound in rags—a large and very well-fed kangaroo. It jumped and moaned, jumped and moaned, and jumped and ... **CRASH!**

Deepu moved cautiously towards where the mummy lay face down on the floor. A light flashed behind him.

Meera crept up, her phone torch held aloft. 'You killed it?' she asked Deepu in awe.

'Erm, it was already dead, Meera.'

'Uff! You know what I mean! You ... knocked it over!'

'Actually, I think it tripped on Vedant.'

"I-I was just tired, okay?" Vedant squeaked.

Meera snorted and moved the phone closer. The bandages around its face had come undone. A pink ear showed through, a nose, a patch of white hair. '**GROAAAR!**' it moaned again, and wriggled about.

Carefully, Deepu reached forward and lifted the cloth away from the mummy's face.

'Is it dead?' Meera asked, rather foolishly.

'I hope not,' said Deepu. 'Because that's Mr Pocha.'

The others gathered around the fallen figure.

'Mr Pocha is a mummy?'

'Mr Pocha is haunting the museum?'

'I thought all mummieth were girlth!'

'Hee! Girlth!'

Anmol shook his head sadly, and reached for another sandwich.

Deepu kneeled down beside Mr Pocha and carefully unwrapped the cloth around his face.

Mr Pocha stared up at him. 'MMPPPFFFF!' he said,

75

through the packing tape stretched tightly over his mouth. 'MGGFF—AAAOOOCH!' Deepu had ripped the tape off. 'Thank you, young man,' he whispered, gasping for breath.

Deepu realised that Mr Pocha wasn't really wrapped in bandages like a mummy. He'd been bound securely with lengths of fabric from Mummy's beloved garment exhibit.

'Mr Pocha, why are you wearing Jodha Bai's sari?'

Then the questions flew, fast and furious.

'Mr Pocha, are you a mummy?'

'Mr Pocha, are you haunting the museum?'

'Mr Pocha, have you been *possessed* by the soul of the mummy?'

'Mither Potha, thouldn't you be a daddy?'

'Hoo! Mither Potha!'

'Mr Pocha, want a sandwich?'

'Mr Pocha, are you stealing things from the museum, dressed as the mummy?' But even as he asked, Deepu couldn't quite believe it. Not sweet, kind old Mr Pocha, who loved the dusty rooms of the museum even more than Mummy and Deepu did.

'Whut!' Mr Pocha yelled. 'No! I'm not ... I wouldn't ... it's those guys!'

'Huh?'

'The guys who tied me up and left me here.'

'Wuh?'

Mr Pocha looked over Meera's shoulder. His eyes widened.

'Those guys!' he whispered, waggling his head in the direction of the door.

'Bwuh?'

'The ones standing behind you!' Mr Pocha hissed. His head waggled harder.

'Hah!' Vedant said. 'That old trick! You can't fool us!'

'HANDS UP!' Someone yelled from behind them.

Meanwhile ...

CLICK! CLICK!

Nani flexed her arms, preparing to shred the ropes around her.

'STOP!' A voice yelled. 'Stop or I'll drop the kid!'

'What!' Nani and Aftab shouted together.

'You heard me!'

'I'll tell Ammi!' Aftab screamed.

77

'You'd injure your brother over a few photographs of me?' Nani asked.

Changez scrunched up his face. 'All right. No, I wouldn't drop him.'

'Good to know,' said Nani.

'But I'll go on TV and say you did! Or that you left him hanging there even when he called you. Or that you left him stranded in a burning building. Or in a tree about to fall in the middle of a rainstorm. Or in a drowning boat on Gadbadnagar Lake. And I'll go on and on and on ...'

'Why?'

'So I can become famous, that's why!' Changez said. 'I'll be on TV! I'll get a real job—reporting, not pouring cups of tea for people all day!'

'You'd do all that by telling lies about me?' Nani peered at him. He twitched and fidgeted, and looked away.

Nani looked over at Aftab. She guessed he'd been bullied into helping his older brother. Then her head snapped around. A jingling! Stronger this time! She looked out over the trees. Something was wrong; trouble was brewing. But she couldn't leave Aftab behind.

'What will it take to make you stop bothering me?' Nani asked.

'An interview!' Changez grinned.

Eleven

Vedant screamed.

Faizal screamed louder!

Meera gasped.

Anmol chewed.

Two men stood in the doorway to the room, dressed as security guards. One reached in and fumbled for the switches. The lights flickered on, making everyone blink.

Nani! Deepu thought. Nani, where are you? Shouldn't her ninja senses have brought her to the museum by now? He looked around at his friends, frozen in fear, at Mr Pocha, trying very hard not to look like he wanted to scream, and at the Gadbadnagar mummy, the mysterious creature at the centre of all this madness, sleeping peacefully in its glass case.

The two men gaped at the little group in the room.

'Gogi, look! Thieves! Just like us!'

'Bablu! You left the door open again!' Gogi snarled. 'How many times have I told you—make sure you lock the door! Bet you left that service door open also!' His enormous moustache bristled with anger. 'And I told you to tie that Pocha fellow up properly with rope, not some old dhoti!'

'And they're really short thieves!'

'They're children, Bablu!'

'Oh.'

Gogi ground his teeth and snarled. 'We'll have to tie them up as well! I'll get some rope! You check them for phones! And don't let them get away!' Gogi strode away down the corridor.

Bablu stood hands outstretched, blocking the doorway. He glared at the children. They glared back.

'So,' he said finally, 'do you have phones?'

'No!' Meera said.

'Yes!' Anmol slapped a hand to his head. THANNNNG! He'd forgotten the tiffin box he was clutching.

Bablu stepped forward, reaching for the phone.

'Don't you dare!' Meera yelled, holding it behind her back. 'I'll ... I'll call the police!'

'Ai, that's my grandpa's phone!' Anmol yelled through a mouthful of bread and cheese, rushing forward.

Bablu flinched, wiped his face and grabbed at the nearest child.

'Pleaaath! Don't beath me!' Faizal shrieked.

'Aargh!' Bablu wiped his face again, and grabbed wildly for Anmol.

'Please don't take my tiffin!' Anmol wailed.

'Uurgh!' Bablu staggered back, both hands to his face and—**THUD!**

'Good job, Vedant!' Meera said. 'Tripping that horrible fellow like that!'

GRAAARGH! Bablu rose, lunging for Deepu.

THANNNNG! Down came Anmol's tiffin box on Bablu's head.

'Run, kids!' Mr Pocha yelled, squirming on the floor. 'Run!'

'Don't leave me!' Vedant wailed, scrambling up from the floor.

The children raced for the door and ...

SPLAT!

... ran straight into Gogi!

'HRAAAARGH!' he snarled, lunging for them.

'EEEEE!' screamed AnuManu!

THWACK! Gogi's eyes crossed as he sank slowly to the ground. The children screamed again, staring wide-eyed at the Rajput warrior looming above them, waving a walking stick ...

Meanwhile, back in the park ...

'What are your hobbies?' Changez read out from his notebook.

Nani blinked. 'Seriously?'

'What is your favourite song?'

'Is this a joke?'

'If you were a cupcake, which flavour of cupcake would you be?'

'Changez, you've got your poor brother hanging from a tree to ask me about cupcakes?'

'It's not my fault,' Changez sniffed. 'That TV reporter set these questions.'

Aftab sniffed, swinging slowly from side to side.

Nani tensed. Her ninja senses were jingling furiously. She had to act fast.

'How did you become a ninja?' Changez asked.

Nani muttered a spell.

'You called?' A sparrow hopped down onto the nets by her shoulder.

'I need help. Distract him for me, please?'

The little bird glared down at Changez. 'It will be my pleasure!' She fluttered away, calling out to her friends.

Something wet and smelly splattered onto Changez's head.

'Ugh!' He wiped at his head. 'Filthy birds!'

PLOP!!

Changez cried out in disgust. What were the birds of Gadbadnagar eating, he thought.

GLOOPETY-FLOOPETY-SHLOOP!

Changez fell back, blinded by the thick, wet slime that covered his face. He flailed at his face, trying to get the vile smelling muck out of his eyes, his nose, his mouth ...

When he opened his eyes, Nani was gone. The net, now just a shredded mess of frayed rope ends, swung faintly in the breeze. Aftab stalked up to him, scowling.

'Just wait till I tell Ammi!' he hissed. 'Just wait!'

From the branches above came a sound like a dozen birds together.

It sounded, Changez thought, like they were laughing ...

The children's screams echoed through the dark corridors, rang out through the deserted rooms, bounced off the old walls, the dusty cabinet cases, swooped down the stairwell and into every corner.

In a dimly lit corridor, two men in security guard uniforms struggled to their feet and stumbled after the children.

In a corner near the water cooler, a dark shadow stiffened in a corner, listening intently. Trouble, he thought, snarling to himself. Trouble with a capital ... **BLARP!**

And in the shadows by the prehistory exhibit in the Main Hall, a figure wrapped in yellowed rags froze and turned ...

GRAAAAOOOON!

Shrieks, laughter, whispers filled the air. But the children barely noticed.

'Not bad for a ninety-three-year-old, eh?' Mr Chitnis cackled as he waved his walking stick about. The helmet from the Rajput exhibit wobbled on his head. The armour he'd slipped on jangled as he swung about, narrowly missing the children flocked around him. 'But what's the rush?'

Deepu held his arm, trying to steer him towards the staircase behind the rest of his classmates.

'They're bad guys, Mr Chitnis. We have to get out of—'

'HYAARGH! COME BACK HERE!' Gogi staggered to his feet.

'Come on!' Meera hissed, leading the small group down the staircase.

Down the end of the corridor was the service door, still ajar. And beyond it, free—

GRAAARH!!

Something loomed out of the shadows! Something wrapped in yellowed rages, its hands reaching out in the dim light, its eyes burning like coals. It roared, lunging at the children.

It was ...

A mummy!

GRAAAOOOOORGH ...

Twelve

Imagine you are a sparrow.

Yes, yes, it is a particularly thrilling bit of the story and you are close to falling off the edge of your seat in nervous excitement. And yes, you have chewed your fingernails all the way down to the ends and are about to start chomping on your toenails. Of course, you need to get back to where the action is.

So stop wasting time, will you? Close your eyes. Now take a deep breath. SHWEEE. Take another. SHWOOO! No peeking!

Ready?

Imagine you are a sparrow flying over Gadbadnagar on this finger-and-toenail-bitingly exciting night.

Well, as you swooped past the aquarium and down the road, you'd probably see a bunch of very tired attendants from the Senior Citizens' Home, scouring the streets for a certain ninety-three-year-old. And further ahead, you'd see a rather battered-looking orange scooter bouncing along, with a very loud fellow bellowing instructions from the pillion seat. The skinny kid driving is doing his best but he just can't seem to go fast enough. That, and he's having trouble seeing through the enormous helmet he's wearing. At length, the scooter wobbles to a stop. The driver gets down, the pillion rider takes over.

And if you were a sparrow with exceptional eyesight, you'd see a shadow that just went—ZIP! ZAP! ZAPOW!— past the statue of Mahatma Gandhi!

In a flash, the scooter takes off, after the shadow. Leaving a skinny young fellow in a SuperAmmi helmet behind.

But there's more—huffing down the pavement is yet another Gadbadnagar citizen who just can't seem to fall asleep tonight.

'But Doraiswami,' our sleepless citizen squawks into a mobile phone, 'I'm sure Mr Pocha called me! I think he's in trouble!'

A deep, dense silence settles on the street, punctuated by feeble squawks from the phone.

'But now his phone has been switched off!'

More squeaks and squawks.

'You're right, it's probably nothing,' the figure says at last. 'He's probably asleep at home, not in the museum.'

The squeaks continue.

The figure stops running and bends over, gasping for breath. Across the road, the museum sits in total darkness, bathed in the soft glow of the streetlamps in the gardens around it.

'Must start working out!' the figure gasps. 'No more excuses. From tomorrow for sure!'

It straightens up to go—and stops. A single window on the first floor suddenly flares with light!

'There's someone inside!'

Thirteen

They were in trouble! Big, big trouble!

Deepu looked around at the rest of his group, now huddled together on the floor in a corner of the prehistory room: seven children, Mr Pocha and a very old Rajput warrior. Bablu was in a corner, mumbling into his phone. Looming over them, waving Mr Chitnis' walking stick, was Gogi. And right behind him—the mummy that had cornered them!

The children gaped as it staggered toward them, with an evil-looking weapon in its hand.

'It wants our eyes!' Meera gasped. 'It's going to stick that thing into us and ... Oh.'

Everyone watched in silence as the mummy stuck the weapon down its bandages and scratched its back. 'Aah!' it sighed. 'What a relief! Gogi, can I keep this backscratcher?'

'Put it down!' Gogi roared. 'It's worth a

lot of money!' He whipped around, glaring at the children. 'Who told you to come here?'

Five trembling fingers pointed at Meera.

'You thieves!' Mr Pocha squealed. 'I know what you're doing! Wait till I get the police!'

'They're going to think you did it!' Bablu laughed. 'We'll make sure of that!'

The mummy reached into the bandages near its hip. A small thermos flask emerged; the children gaped as the mummy shook it menacingly at them.

'Why are you here? Answer me!' Gogi yelled.

But the children's eyes were riveted on the mummy raising its flask to its lips.

'SHLUUURP!' The mummy sucked noisily at the flask. A sickly green stain spread around its mouth.

'It's ... it's drinking its kidneys!' Meera gasped. 'Like a milkshake!'

'TCHEE!' 'Yuck!' 'SHEEE!' 'Mummy!'

'Who told you to come here?' Gogi snarled, waving the stick about to get their attention.

'SHLOOOORP!' The mummy took another sip.

'It's coming to life!' Meera screamed. Vedant and Mr Pocha joined in.

'Err, it already has,' Deepu said.

Meera turned to him, looking more excited than fearful. 'They take all its organs out before it gets mummified, right? So maybe it's drinking its organs back bit by bit, for, like, energy, or something!'

Meera and Deepu stared at each other for a horrified instant.

'Awesome!' they both beamed.

'I said, who ...'

'SHLEEEERP!' The mummy seemed to be sucking the last bits of its kidneys out of the flask. It wiped its mouth with the back of one bandaged hand, spreading green goo all over its face.

'You and your crazy diets, Elvis!' Gogi snarled. 'You're driving me crazy!'

'I need it to keep my strength up,' the mummy drawled. 'Gogi, you should try it too, yaar!'

Gogi shuddered.

'I knew it!' Meera hissed. 'You're drinking your kidneys and lungs!'

Everyone gasped, even Gogi. Even the mummy.

'What? Tchee, no!' the mummy shuddered. 'How gross! Yuck!'

'Then, what ... ?' Anmol pointed a trembling finger at the empty bottle in his hand.

'This? It's a spinach-mint-karela smoothie. Gives me strength. Builds immunity. Good for complexion also! Mummy's special recipe!' Everyone shuddered again.

'I meant *my* mummy,' explained the mummy.

'Ha!' Gogi snorted. 'Strength for what? All you have to do is roam around, moaning and making sure no one enters the building!'

'Oh, yeah! You do it then, if you think it's so easy!' Elvis whined.

'You bet it's easy! I have to carry heavy stuff, coordinate the pick-up, talk to the boss *and* manage this Bablu!'

Bablu frowned, then turned away to answer his phone.

'Hah! That's nothing! I can't sit even sit properly, these band-aids are so tight!' Elvis whined.

'Bandages!' Gogi and Meera hissed together.

'And they're so itchy! I have this horrible rash all over my ...'

'Ew!' everyone squealed.

'And do you know how much trouble all these band-aids are when I have to ... you know, go?' Elvis waggled his head wildly to the side.

'Go where?' Gogi glared at him.

'You know, the little boys' room!' Though every inch of him was covered, Deepu was sure Elvis had blushed as he said that.

KHRAAAARGH!

Everyone jumped. But it was only Mr Chitnis enjoying a quick nap.

Bablu returned. 'Boss not happy!' he said in a low voice. 'He said wind up and finish, so I said, yes-boss, okay-boss, but what to do with the old Rajput?'

Gogi winced. 'What did he say?'

'Several rude things about my brain size,' Bablu sulked. 'Really hurt my feelings. So I told him I was glad I hadn't mentioned the children.'

'What did he say then?'

'Oh, nothing.'

'Eh?'

'He only screamed.'

'Excuse me, uncle. I have to go,' Anmol piped up.

'Eh?'

'Little boys' room.'

'I also.' 'Me too.' 'I altho!' 'Yes, yes, me too.' Even Mr Pocha joined in.

'What!' Gogi quavered. 'No!'

'Uncle, please!' 'Urgent it is!' 'Pleath!'

Gogi's phone rang.

'Quiet! Quiet!' Gogi yelped.

QUiET!

Pin-drop silence filled the room.

'Stop helping them, Meera!' Deepu hissed.

'Sorry,' she shrugged. 'Force of habit.'

Gogi put away his phone. 'That was the boss,' he said. 'We're taking the kids!'

Pongo?

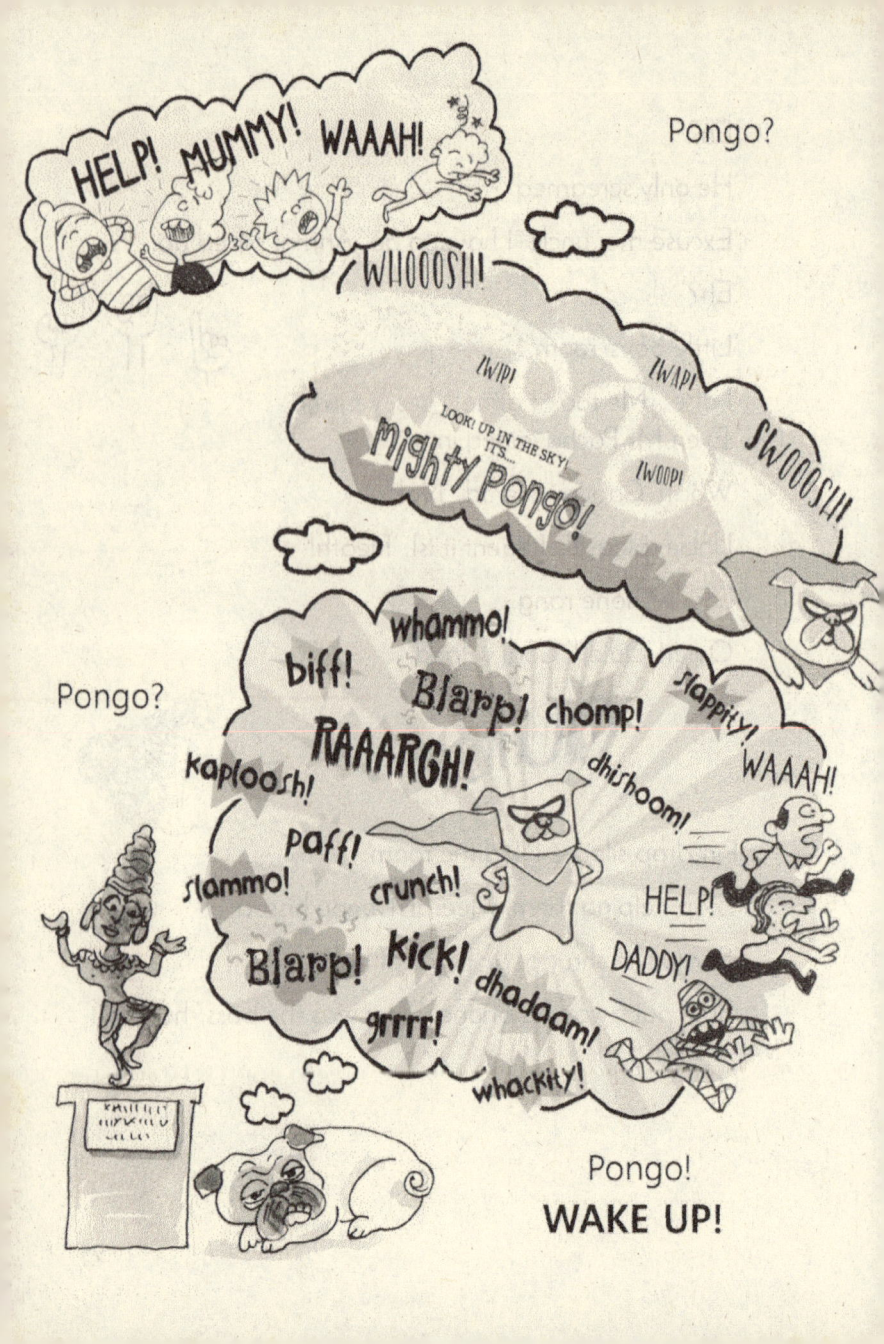

Pongo?

Pongo!
WAKE UP!

Fourteen

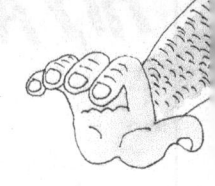

'No! No!' Vedant screamed.

'Leave them alone, you devils!' Mr Pocha squawked.

'Aliens!' Mr Chitnis screeched, waking with a start.

Gogi stretched one hairy arm towards Deepu ...

A voice rings out through the room.

'NOT SO FAST, YOU CHICKPEAS!'

And this time, it's not a fake mummy (or a mummy that is someone's mummy, or a fake mummy's smoothie-making mummy or a mummy that was once someone's daddy).

It's not a schoolkid with a sandwich ...

It's definitely not a blarping, yip-yapping dog.

It's ...

HIYAAAAAAAAAA!

MYSTERY HERO!

NANI!

HAHAHAHAHAHA!
HOOHOOHOOHOOH
HEEHEEHEEHEEHEE

HAI! HUP! HYO!

YOU KNOW WHAT HAPPENS NEXT.

hishoom!
dhadaam!
biff!
thud!
HAI!
whammo!
slappity!
paf!
HUP!
kaploosh!
kick!
HYO!
whackity!

HAIIIIIIIIIIIIIIIIIIIIIII!
EEEEEEEEEEEEE
AIIIYOOOOOOOO!

'Take cover!' Meera yelled, diving under a table, rolling over and then crawling commando-style across the floor. The others watched, in stunned silence, as she scooted across the floor on her elbows to a door in the far corner, peeked behind it, then gave them a curt nod and a thumbs up.

A minute later, seven children found themselves crammed into a small storeroom. They stood there, listening to the thuds, groans and screams from the hall outside. A moment later, a small chewing noise joined the chorus.

'Honestly, Anmol,' Meera hissed 'How much tiffin did you bring?'

THUD! GRUNT! DHADAAM!

Deepu reached for the wall and fumbled around until a dim light flickered on.

CRASH! BASH! HIYAAA!

'Mummy!' Vedant whimpered.

CRASH! The door flew open.

Light flooded in!

AAAH! The kids screamed for there, standing in the doorway was ... a mummy!

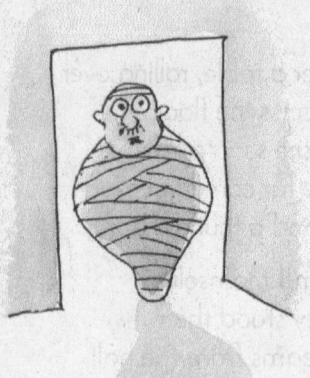

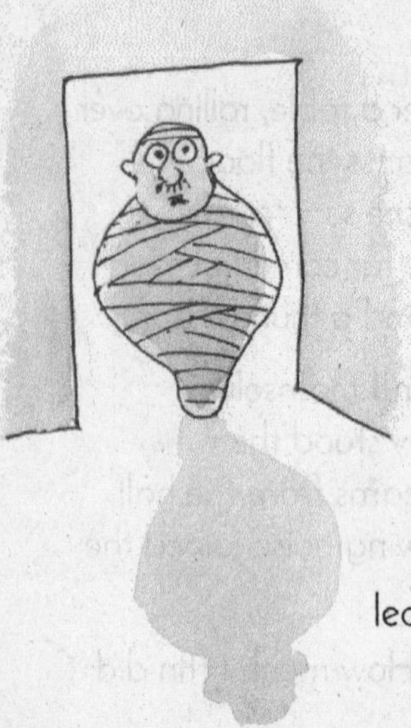

The children shrank back in fear as the mummy lunged forward and ...

BOING! BOING! BOING!

... hopped in to the room with them.

Deepu drew the door shut after Mr Pocha.

'Are you all right, kids?' he panted, leaning against the wall.

'Yes.' 'Yes.' 'Yes.'

Things whammed and crashed and thudded outside.

'Daddy!' Vedant wailed.

CRASH! The door flew open!

Light flooded in!

AAAH! The kids screamed for there, standing in the doorway was ... a Rajput warrior!

'Ah! The gang's all here!' Mr Chitnis giggled as he shuffled in, his helmet wobbling wildly on his head.

'Such a scare I got!' Faizal breathed.

'I know!' 'Me too!' 'I swear!'

'Hey, Faizal,' Deepu whispered. 'You're not lisping anymore!'

'Yeah,' Faizal grinned. 'I don't really need to.'

'So why ...'

Faizal grinned. 'People keep ducking,' he explained. 'It's funny!'

Deepu leaned over. 'And AnuManu seem to enjoy it too.'

'Shh!' Faizal hissed, blushing. Then, sneaking a quick look across the room, he added, 'Really?'

'Mummy!' Vedant whimpered again.

BASH! The door flew open!

Light flooded in!

'AAAAAAH!' There, in the doorway, stood ... a mummy!

103

The children shrank back as it reached in and pulled ...

... a flask out of the bandages around its waist.

SHAKE! SHAKE! SHLOOORP! SHLUURP! BURP!

'YEAAARGH!' Mr Chitnis leaped forward, his walking stick held high. But the mummy calmly reached up and grabbed the stick away. Deepu lunged at his legs. Elvis reached down and lifted the boy off.

'I told you that smoothie kept my energy up!' he smirked.

Then, grinning an evil, green grin, he tightened his grip on Deepu's collar and reached for Faizal ...

THANNNG! A Maratha spittoon flew through the door and landed squarely on Elvis' head. He slid down to the ground with a groan and stayed there.

'AAAAAAA!' the children screamed. There in the doorway, stood ... a mummy!

104

'AAAAAAAA!' the mummy screamed back.

Then, it reached in, grabbed Deepu and ...

... squashed him in a great big, bear hug!

'Deepu! Why are you here?' the mummy screamed, squeezing him even tighter. 'Why are you all here? Didn't I tell you to be in bed by ten? Did you eat? Really? Did you brush? Really? Did you do soosoo bef—'

'Mummy, focus!' Deepu yelled.

It was a mummy. Deepu's.

'Mr Pocha!' Mummy gasped, looking around at the rest of the people in the room. 'Why are you wearing Razia Sultan's battle turban? Mr Chitnis, put Rana Pratap's helmet down this instant! And why are all you kids even here?'

'Those villains are looting our museum!' Mr Pocha said. 'They're taking our old coins, the knives from the Maratha room, the backscratchers, even the mummy!'

'The chaddi-banian exhibit!' Mummy gasped. 'Is it safe?'

Mr Pocha looked at her strangely. 'The historic garments, you mean? I think they've taken some of those too.'

Things—and people—continued to fly about outside. Mummy cautiously opened the door.

'Is that Pongo?' Mummy gasped. 'My god, it is!'

Mummy stared out, then froze.

'And is that the Mystery Hero?' she said.

Nani screeched to a halt in the doorway of the storeroom. She stared at Mummy. Mummy stared back.

Then Nani backflipped away.

Mummy turned to Deepu, her eyes wide. 'That sweatshirt!' she whispered. 'Those tights! That scarf!'

Oh no! Had Mummy recognised Nani?

Mummy beamed. 'I have the exact same clothes too!' she squeaked. 'Same-same!'

'Is there anything else you noticed?' Deepu asked carefully.

'Hmm?' Mummy said absently. 'What was that, beta?'

'Nothing,' Deepu grinned. 'Nothing at all.'

106

Fifteen

Everyone trooped out into the Main Hall. It was a shambles, with backscratchers, cooking vessels and historic underpants lying everywhere. Mummy— after a quick inspection, and a bit of earsplitting 'HOOLOOLOOLOO'ing—announced that things weren't too bad. A few cabinets had been broken, and a lot of the fake fossils would have to be replaced. Most of the display cases had been stripped clean, but their contents were all found in a big heap of sacks in one corner.

The children huddled together, gaping at a different exhibit: Gogi, Bablu and Elvis, tied up and unconscious in the middle of the floor.

'The Superknot!' Vedant gasped. 'The Mark of the Mystery Hero! It's humanly impossible to open it!'

Deepu hid his smile; only two people knew how easy the knot was to unravel and he just happened to be one of them.

'Quite an adventure, eh?' a voice said. Everyone cheered wildly and rushed up to exchange high-fives with the famous Mystery Hero.

RAARGH! Pongo sprang out from behind a marble bust of Chanakya. He glared around the room at all the two-legged trouble standing in it. Then Nani stepped forward.

'Good job, Pongo!' she said. And then, in a voice only the little dog could hear, she added, 'Or should I say, Mighty Pongo?'

A look seemed to pass between them.

'Is everyone all right?' a voice called out.

'Ah! There's Doraiswami!' Mummy said.

Doraiswami rushed in through the door of the Main Hall, the tiny hairy tower on his head jiggling with every step. He looked wildly around the room and rushed from one corner of the room to another, exclaiming loudly at the mess and squealing in horror as he peered into the sacks full of stolen loot. Deepu watched as he reached into his pocket and shook the bottle into his hands. A sharp, sweet smell filled his nostrils; a dry rustle followed.

'Unbelievable!' Doraiswami gasped. 'Just three men fooled a whole town, and nearly robbed this museum!' He walked over to the three bound men, seemed to stumble near Gogi, and got back on his feet. On the wall beside him, his shadow wobbled and straightened with him, the pointy tower of his hair resembling a cap. Deepu's eyes widened.

'Four,' said Deepu.

'Eh?'

'Four people tried to rob the museum,' Deepu said. 'There was a fourth one that they called boss.'

'Did you call the police, Dorai?' Mr Pocha asked, leaning against a cabinet. No one had thought to untie the museum director's bandages, not even Mr Pocha himself.

'Yes, yes!' Doriswami said, his hands in his pockets. 'In fact, I'm going to go get them myself.' He turned.

'It's him!' Deepu yelled. 'Doraiswami is the boss!'

'That's rubbish!' laughed Doraiswami. 'Let me go get the police, they'll straighten everything.'

'Mystery Hero!' Deepu yelled.

ZWOOSH! Nani was already flying across the room.

'Not so fast!' she said, landing lightly in front of Doraiswami. He tried to duck around Nani.

ZIP! ZWOOP! Nani blocked him each time. SWOOP!

'He's got Gogi's phone!' Deepu shouted. 'Dorai was calling him all night. You'll find all those calls on their phones!'

Doraiswami lunged around Nani. SWOOOSH! In one smooth move, she caught him, tossed him in the air and caught him by the legs as he descended headfirst. Things rained out of his pockets as he hung in the air, upside down—coins, a comb, a bottle of sanitiser, and two phones.

Nani set Doraiswami down, one hand still firmly on his shoulder.

'Dorai, how could you!' Mr Pocha thundered. 'My museum! My life's work! How could you!'

'And I bet you didn't call the police!' Mummy said. 'You were planning to escape, weren't you, right after you took that phone. So no one would connect you to this robbery.'

With one desperate lunge, Doraiswami wrenched himself out of Nani's grip and threw himself at the two children closest to him—Faizal and Anmol!

'Stand back!' he shrieked, pulling the two boys roughly forward, like human shields. 'Stand back or else ...'

Grabbing each child by the collar, he dragged them closer and stumbled backwards, towards the main doors.

'Uncle!' Faizal screamed, inches from Doraiswami's ear. 'Pleath don'th thake me!'

Doraiswami staggered back, losing his grip on Faizal as he wiped frantically at his face.

'Uncle!' Anmol screamed in his other ear, half a cutlet hanging from his mouth. 'Don't take my snacks!'

Doraiswami gasped and let go of Anmol, both hands to his face. He whirled around, searching feverishly in his pockets, and bumped into Vedant.

HYAAANCHOOOO!

'Sorry!' Vedant sniffed, as Doraiswami staggered back, squealing and clawing at his face.

'Looking for this, Dorai?' Mummy asked. A little bottle gleamed in her hand—the sanitiser Nani had shaken out of his pockets.

Doraiswami looked wildly around the room—at Mummy, at Nani, at the three thieves, at the bags of loot he'd nearly gotten away with. Then he spun around, dashed for the door and ...

'AAAAIIIII!' he screamed—

As he was brought down by a mummy.

Not the real mummy, still peacefully in its glass case ...

Not Elvis, the smoothie-drinking mummy, who was halfway across the room and unconscious ...

Not Deepu's mummy, not even Deepu's Mummy's mummy ...

It was Mr Pocha who—BOING! BOING! BOING!—had hopped across the room and landed, with a great **THUD**, right on top of Doraiswami.

'I've called the police!' Mummy said, a moment later, putting away her phone.

'Good work, everyone!' Nani said, standing beside Mr Pocha, who was still sitting on top of his assistant. 'Now if you will all gather here before me ...'

112

Soon, six children, two mummies and one crook with a fear of germs found themselves growing sleepier, their minds lighter, their memories hazier. Slowly, gently, the Mindblur eased itself into their heads, coaxed their tired brains into believing they hadn't seen Nani, lulled them into letting go of everything but the vaguest memories of her ...

The Mindblur complete, Nani stepped back.

'Sorry, Meera,' Deepu muttered as he wiped out all the photographs she'd taken that night. Well, almost all of them.

Deepu pressed a few buttons, looked up guiltily at Nani, then deleted every trace of the last photograph from the phone in his hand. Across town, a phone beeped, tucked away under a pillow in an empty bed.

'The police will be here any minute,' Nani said. 'We should head out.'

'Will they be all right?' Deepu looked anxiously at his friends.

'Oh yes,' Nani smiled. 'I have someone special watching over them.' In his corner, Pongo bowed his head.

CRAAAASH! Something shiny and orange burst in through the main doors and skidded to a wobbly stop in the middle of the room.

'Now what?' sighed Nani.

A loud, nasal voice brayed, 'Aunty! SAY CHEESE!'

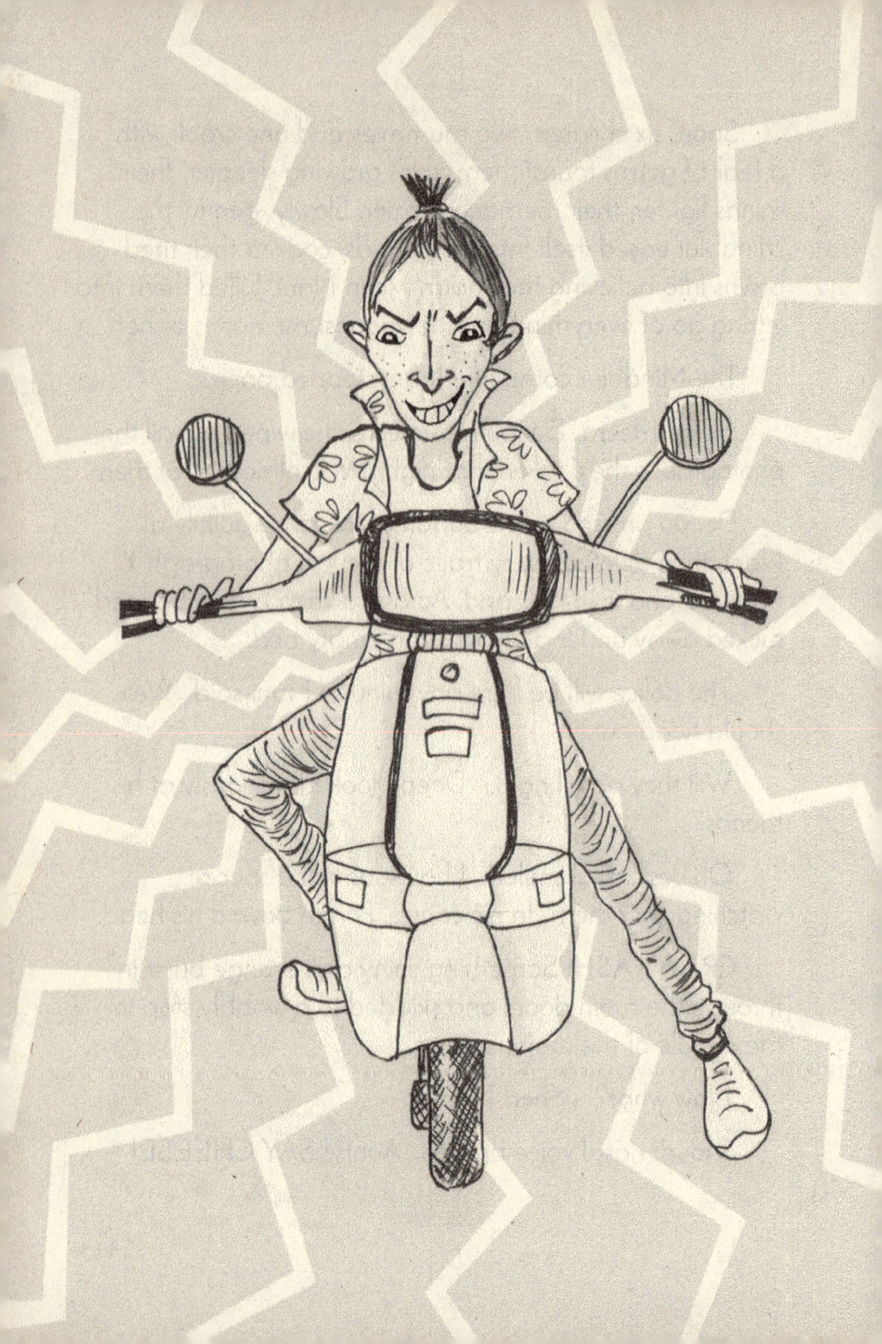

Sixteen

'I've had enough of you,' Nani said, her voice low but firm.

Changez ignored her, bounding about the room taking photographs of everything. He took pictures of the children, of Mr Pocha, of Mummy, of the four captured thieves.

Then he zoomed in on Deepu.

'Leave him alone, Changez!' Nani said.

'Nani!' Deepu yelled, as he tried to avoid the flashing camera.

'Nani! That's interesting!' Changez sniggered. 'Now I'll crack your identity even faster, Mystery Hero!'

A skinny boy in an oversized orange helmet ran in through the door.

'Changez bhai! Stop it! Enough!'

YIP! YAP! RAARGH! Someone small and furious rushed out from behind a display case, straight at Changez.

But the reporter deftly dodged Pongo's attack, hopping over and around the little dog with admirable grace. He hopped, he skipped—he even pirouetted!

'He took ballet in school,' Aftab said mournfully. 'He can bounce around for hours!'

'Hah! Can't catch me-e!' Changez sang. **CLICK! CLICK! CLICK!**

Nani smiled. She moved into the centre of the room, put her palms together and closed her eyes.

'What's this? A battle stance? Some sort of ninja asana? Ooh, I'm so scared!' Changez gleefully continued taking pictures.

Nani opened her eyes. 'You should be,' she smiled. Then, lifting her fingers to her mouth, she whistled. PHWEEEEEEET!

Changez lowered his camera. 'That's it? That's all you're going to do?'

'Uh-huh.'

Something fluttered in through the window—a sparrow.

'What, a single whistle?' Changez sneered.

'That's right.'

There was more movement, more fluttering.

'Bhai,' Aftab's voice quavered. 'Stop it now.'

CLICK! CLICK! CLICK!

GLOOP! Something wet and smelly landed on his head. He looked up. A bright-eyed pigeon looked down at him from the top of a light fitting.

'Not again!' he said, then stopped. For there was a crow. And a mynah. And ...

Changez yelped. Perched on every cupboard, table and light fixture in the room, were birds. Lots of them. All sitting silently, with their bright beady eyes fixed—on him.

Nani nodded.

In one fluid movement, the birds swooped off their perches and shot across the room, straight at Changez.

The reporter screamed, as a wave of birds engulfed him. He flailed about with his arms, his camera swinging from the strap around his neck, as the birds whirred and cheeped and flapped in a tornado of feathers around him.

Deepu watched, wide-eyed in horror. Pongo dived under a cabinet and stayed there.

'They're eating him!' Aftab screamed, his hands clasped to his face. 'They're tearing him into little bits and pecking at him and gobbling him up and ... Oh.'

As abruptly as the birds had arrived, they left, swooping up and out of the window in perfect coordination.

Changez stood in the middle of the room, covered in feathers and bird poo, but otherwise unhurt.

'Hah!' He tossed his head back in a shower of bird droppings. 'Couldn't do a thing to me!'

Then he frowned, looking first at Deepu, then Nani, then at Aftab.

'What?' he demanded. 'What are you three grinning at?'

Aftab just smiled and shook his head.

'What?' Changez snapped again. Then he looked down at his hands and found his answer.

His camera was gone.

From Deepu's Top-secret Ninja Nani Scrapbook

First mummy, now dada:
Senior citizen prowls museum, seeking aliens

Mummy spills beans
Gangmember Elvis reveals museum robbery plans: Rumours, trickery used to scare town!

Mummy spins yarn
Mayor's mummy enthrals crowds at Gadbadnagar Storytelling Festival

Poop attack!
US Army studying ways to use bird poop in warfare

Museum mummy mystery solved!

Superknot, confused thieves: Was Mystery Hero our secret saviour — again?

Chadd-tees make history

Museum gift shop reports record- breaking sales

Sleeping kids, scary dog:
Surprise find in museum store

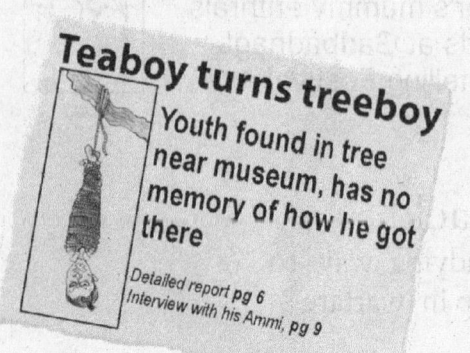

Teaboy turns treeboy

Youth found in tree near museum, has no memory of how he got there

Detailed report pg 6
Interview with his Ammi, pg 9

Photograph received on Deepu's phone

W T
O U
B T

Third note found nailed to front door!

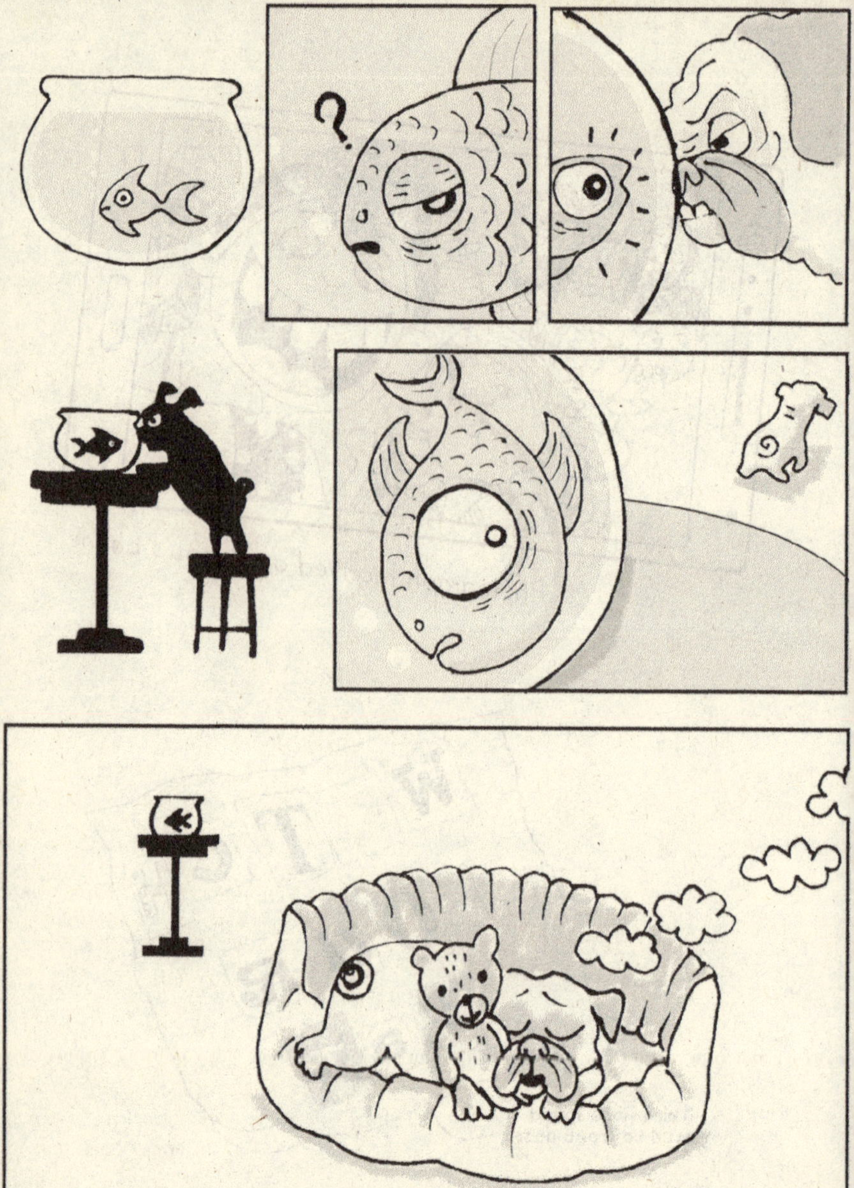

ZZZZT!

Lavanya Karthik is a Mighty and Most Excellent Warrior of the Light, leading an army of ninja against the Loathsome Hordes, but only in her dreams. In real life, she lives in Mumbai where she writes, draws, eats way too much chocolate and takes a lot of naps. She does lead an army, though, of imaginary pugs.